VMware Virtual SAN Cookbook

The perfect guide to successful VMware Virtual SAN implementation and operations, with recipes to guide you through the process

Jeffrey Taylor

PUBLISHING

BIRMINGHAM - MUMBAI

VMware Virtual SAN Cookbook

First published: August 2015

Production reference: 1270815

Published by Packt Publishing Ltd.
Livery Place
35 Livery Street
Birmingham B3 2PB, UK.

ISBN 978-1-78217-454-7

www.packtpub.com

Credits

Author
Jeffrey Taylor

Reviewers
Chris M Evans
Charbel Nemnom
Vladan SEGET

Commissioning Editor
Ashwin Nair

Acquisition Editor
James Jones

Content Development Editor
Anish Sukumaran

Technical Editors
Namrata Patil
Tanmayee Patil

Copy Editors
Tani Kothari
Angad Singh

Project Coordinator
Mary Alex

Proofreader
Safis Editing

Indexer
Rekha Nair

Graphics
Jason Monteiro

Production Coordinator
Aparna Bhagat

Cover Work
Aparna Bhagat

About the Author

Jeffrey Taylor is an IT professional with deep knowledge of VMware vSphere and storage infrastructures. He has been working with VMware's global support services for nearly 5 years and is currently a staff engineer with a focus on Virtual SAN and storage infrastructure. Before his current role, he worked on a variety of software platforms for a global financial processor, with an emphasis on Unix/Linux midrange systems and mission-critical distributed applications.

About the Reviewers

Chris M Evans has worked in the IT industry for over 27 years. After receiving a BSc (Hons) in computational science and mathematics from the University of Leeds, his early IT career started in mainframe and followed both systems programming and storage paths. During the dot-com boom, he also cofounded and successfully floated a company that sold music and digital downloads. For most of the last 20 years, Chris has worked as an independent consultant, focusing on open systems storage, and more recently, virtualization and cloud. He has worked in industry verticals including finance, transport, utilities, retail, designing, deploying, and managing storage infrastructures for all major vendors. In addition to his consultancy work, Chris writes a widely read and respected blog, `http://blog.architecting.it`, and produces articles for online publications. He has also been featured in numerous podcasts as a guest and content provider.

Charbel Nemnom is a Microsoft Most Valuable Professional (MVP) for Hyper-V and technical evangelist with 5nine Software. He has extensive infrastructure expertise and a lot of knowledge of a variety of Microsoft and VMware technologies. He has over 13 years of professional experience in the information technology field and in guiding technical teams to optimize the performance of mission-critical enterprise systems. He has worked as a system and network engineer, senior consultant, and IT manager and has a history of successful enterprise projects in the IT, banking, education, and publishing sectors. He works as a virtualization consultant architect in the MENA region. He coauthored *Hyper-V Best Practices*, *Packt Publishing*.

Charbel also runs his blog at `https://charbelnemnom.com`, where he writes frequently about software-defined data center and cloud computing.

Charbel has certifications from Microsoft, Cisco, and VMware and holds these credentials: VCA-DCV, MCP, MCSA, MCTS, MCITP, MCS, MCSE, CCNP, ITIL®, and PMP®. You can follow him on Twitter at `@CharbelNemnom`.

I would like to extend a big thank you to my family, especially to my wife, Ioana, for her support and patience throughout this project. She is the reason I can fulfill my dream and follow my passion.

Last but not least, I want to thank the Packt Publishing team for supporting all the authors and reviewers during this project.

Vladan SEGET is as an independent consultant, professional blogger, vExpert, VCAP5-DCA/DCD, and VCP 4/5. His blog, an ESX virtualization site, which can be found at `http://www.vladan.fr/`, was started as a simple bookmarking site but quickly found a large following of readers and subscribers. Today, it's one of the leading virtualization blogs.

www.PacktPub.com

Support files, eBooks, discount offers, and more

For support files and downloads related to your book, please visit www.PacktPub.com.

Did you know that Packt offers eBook versions of every book published, with PDF and ePub files available? You can upgrade to the eBook version at www.PacktPub.com and as a print book customer, you are entitled to a discount on the eBook copy. Get in touch with us at service@packtpub.com for more details.

At www.PacktPub.com, you can also read a collection of free technical articles, sign up for a range of free newsletters and receive exclusive discounts and offers on Packt books and eBooks.

https://www2.packtpub.com/books/subscription/packtlib

Do you need instant solutions to your IT questions? PacktLib is Packt's online digital book library. Here, you can search, access, and read Packt's entire library of books.

Why subscribe?

- ▸ Fully searchable across every book published by Packt
- ▸ Copy and paste, print, and bookmark content
- ▸ On demand and accessible via a web browser

Free access for Packt account holders

If you have an account with Packt at www.PacktPub.com, you can use this to access PacktLib today and view 9 entirely free books. Simply use your login credentials for immediate access.

Instant updates on new Packt books

Get notified! Find out when new books are published by following @PacktEnterprise on Twitter or the *Packt Enterprise* Facebook page.

Table of Contents

Preface

VMware Virtual SAN (VSAN) is the converged storage solution for VMware vSphere.

Integrated directly into the hypervisor, this is a native solution with no VM-based intermediaries for storage delivery. As a result, VSAN is fast, simple to deploy and manage, and integrates tightly with the existing VMware vSphere product suite.

As the solution is native to ESXi and runs on the hypervisor itself, its architecture is simplified and the storage-delivery mechanism is tightly integrated and uniquely suited to the needs of vSphere infrastructures. VSAN is an object-oriented storage solution, where each VM is comprised of a number of objects physically distributed across the ESXi cluster. This object-oriented nature means that access to your data happens natively, without the need for traditional intermediate storage protocols like iSCSI or Fibre Channel.

VSAN's object-oriented nature also means that your VMs exist as a series of distributed objects rather than a series of monolithic files. Whereas, with traditional storage, you have a series of files (configuration files, virtual disks, swap, snapshots, and so on), with VSAN you have a coordinated and related series of objects. These objects are a container for small configuration files (the namespace object, also called VM Home), objects for each virtual disk, objects for each snapshot, and an object for the VM swap space.

The key point when discussing VSAN's architecture, is how it integrates into the existing hypervisor infrastructure to deliver the final service of any hypervisor: production virtual machines. Behind this integration of the storage and compute virtualization layers is the notion of hyper-converged infrastructure. VSAN is one element of converged infrastructure. The goal of hyper-converged infrastructure is to abstract the traditional demarcations within the environment (compute, network, and storage) by converging all aspects of the datacenter into a software-defined model with a centralized control plane and a distributed data/IO plane.

VSAN is the storage element of the software-defined datacenter. User data (VMs) is abstracted and distributed across the compute cluster. Each VM exists as a collection of related objects, distributed optimally within the compute resources. VSAN natively integrates with vCenter and its associated management tools. As a result, VSAN brings truly native, truly integrated management of the storage system into the existing and familiar vSphere operating structure.

A major benefit to this new operating model of the storage system is its simplicity and centralized management. VSAN obviates the need for traditional monolithic storage arrays connected via traditional protocols. It also significantly improves on existing virtualization-centric distributed storage solutions, typically delivered as virtual storage appliances (VSAs). Embedding the distributed storage system into the hypervisor allows for gains in performance and management. Native management through the vCenter Server means that storage for the virtual infrastructure can now be deployed and managed by the virtualization engineer.

What this book covers

Chapter 1, Hardware Selection for Your VSAN Cluster, provides guidance on how to build your own VSAN cluster hardware, or how to select from a VSAN Ready Node.

Chapter 2, Initial Configuration and Validation of Your VSAN Cluster, provides the step-by-step procedure to configure your new VSAN cluster and ensure that it is working properly.

Chapter 3, Storage Policy-based Management, introduces the concept of policy-based management, outlines how and why it is useful, and shows how to implement and use storage policies.

Chapter 4, Monitoring VSAN, outlines how to monitor the VSAN cluster following deployment and into production.

Chapter 5, VSAN Maintenance Operations, describes how VSAN maintenance is performed, from cluster expansion to patching to modifying virtual machines.

Chapter 6, Ruby vSphere Console, covers the VSAN-related aspects of the powerful RVC utility that is bundled with the vCenter Server.

Chapter 7, Troubleshooting VSAN, discusses how to identify and resolve various problems that may occur in the Virtual SAN environment.

Chapter 8, Support Success, should you need to contact VMware Support to pursue issue resolution, this chapter sets you up for success by outlining the steps you should take to ensure a smooth and rapid support engagement.

Chapter 9, VSAN 6.0, covers specific changes in VSAN 6.0 and calls out procedural differences between VSAN 6.0 and VSAN 5.5.

Appendix A, Chapter-specific Expansion, highlights a number of VSAN concepts that we discussed throughout this book, which can be expanded with supplementary information to improve comprehension. This information is presented on a chapter-by-chapter basis.

Appendix B, Additional VSAN Information, highlights additional technical details about Virtual SAN and provides information about useful third-party tools.

What you need for this book

For this book to be meaningful and useful, you should have a VMware vSphere infrastructure that you wish to enhance with Virtual SAN, or a plan to deploy Virtual SAN in your computing environment. The typical vSphere utilities, such as a web browser and Adobe Flash Player, are required. Additionally, you will need an SSH client to access ESXi hosts and/or the vCenter Server command lines.

Who this book is for

This book is for administrators of the VMware vSphere infrastructure who want to simplify storage delivery by integrating storage into vSphere. No extensive storage background is needed as VMware Virtual SAN integrates into the existing vSphere solutions, with which you are already familiar.

Sections

In this book, you will find several headings that appear frequently (Getting ready, How to do it, How it works, There's more, and See also).

To give clear instructions on how to complete a recipe, we use these sections as follows:

Getting ready

This section tells you what to expect in the recipe, and describes how to set up any software or any preliminary settings required for the recipe.

How to do it...

This section contains the steps required to follow the recipe.

How it works...

This section usually consists of a detailed explanation of what happened in the previous section.

There's more...

This section consists of additional information about the recipe in order to make the reader more knowledgeable about the recipe.

See also

This section provides helpful links to other useful information for the recipe.

Conventions

In this book, you will find a number of text styles that distinguish between different kinds of information. Here are some examples of these styles and an explanation of their meaning.

Code words in text, database table names, folder names, filenames, file extensions, pathnames, dummy URLs, user input, and Twitter handles are shown as follows: "This will usually begin with naa., but depending on your storage controller type, it could also begin with mpx., t10., or eui."

A block of code is set as follows:

```
[default]
exten => s,1,Dial(Zap/1|30)
exten => s,2,Voicemail(u100)
exten => s,102,Voicemail(b100)
exten => i,1,Voicemail(s0)
```

Any command-line input or output is written as follows:

```
# esxcli storage core claiming reclaim --device naa.6000c29580eef5fec51c9
84a7a662bbc
```

New terms and **important words** are shown in bold. Words that you see on the screen, for example, in menus or dialog boxes, appear in the text like this: "Examine the registered storage providers. There should be a group for **vsanDatastore**."

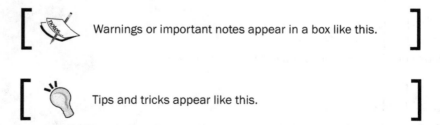

[Warnings or important notes appear in a box like this.]

[Tips and tricks appear like this.]

Reader feedback

Feedback from our readers is always welcome. Let us know what you think about this book—what you liked or disliked. Reader feedback is important for us as it helps us develop titles that you will really get the most out of.

To send us general feedback, simply e-mail `feedback@packtpub.com`, and mention the book's title in the subject of your message.

If there is a topic that you have expertise in and you are interested in either writing or contributing to a book, see our author guide at `www.packtpub.com/authors`.

Customer support

Now that you are the proud owner of a Packt book, we have a number of things to help you to get the most from your purchase.

Errata

Although we have taken every care to ensure the accuracy of our content, mistakes do happen. If you find a mistake in one of our books—maybe a mistake in the text or the code—we would be grateful if you could report this to us. By doing so, you can save other readers from frustration and help us improve subsequent versions of this book. If you find any errata, please report them by visiting `http://www.packtpub.com/submit-errata`, selecting your book, clicking on the **Errata Submission Form** link, and entering the details of your errata. Once your errata are verified, your submission will be accepted and the errata will be uploaded to our website or added to any list of existing errata under the Errata section of that title.

To view the previously submitted errata, go to `https://www.packtpub.com/books/content/support` and enter the name of the book in the search field. The required information will appear under the **Errata** section.

Piracy

Piracy of copyrighted material on the Internet is an ongoing problem across all media. At Packt, we take the protection of our copyright and licenses very seriously. If you come across any illegal copies of our works in any form on the Internet, please provide us with the location address or website name immediately so that we can pursue a remedy.

Please contact us at `copyright@packtpub.com` with a link to the suspected pirated material.

We appreciate your help in protecting our authors and our ability to bring you valuable content.

Questions

If you have a problem with any aspect of this book, you can contact us at questions@ packtpub.com, and we will do our best to address the problem.

1

Hardware Selection for Your VSAN Cluster

In this chapter, we will discuss the following topics, with a recipe for each:

- ▶ Using the VMware Compatibility Guides
- ▶ Selecting a server platform
- ▶ Selecting a storage controller
- ▶ Selecting a solid-state drive (SSD) for the cache tier
- ▶ Selecting hard disk drives/magnetic disks
- ▶ Deciding on a network standard
- ▶ Choosing a VSAN Ready Node (an alternative option)

Introduction

VSAN can only be as good as the hardware on which it runs. VSAN has special requirements for its hardware, and so elements of your VSAN hardware will need to be selected against a stricter subset of the overall VMware Compatibility Guide. Each element of your future VSAN node will need to be compliant with the vSphere and VSAN Compatibility Guides to be production-ready and ensure that the configuration will be supported by VMware.

Depending on your specific needs, you may find that the VSAN Ready Node will better fit your needs. VSAN Ready Nodes are preconfigured systems built by the VMware hardware partners to be VSAN ready, so the machines can simply be purchased and deployed.

You will need to decide whether specifying your own system configuration, or selecting a VSAN Ready Node, is the best choice for your infrastructure. This chapter will prepare you for either choice. VSAN Ready Nodes are covered in the last recipe in this chapter.

Using the VMware Compatibility Guides

While most system vendors offer hardware that is compatible with VMware vSphere, only a subset of the hardware in the VMware Compatibility Guide is applicable for use for VSAN. It is important to make sure that all applicable hardware exists in both guides. The storage-specific components like hard-disk controllers and disks must meet the more-exhaustive performance and reliability requirements for VSAN.

Getting ready

You should have some idea of your hardware requirements. This includes an estimate of your needs for system memory (RAM), along with processor power, networking needs, and storage requirements in terms of capacity and performance.

How to do it...

Go to your web browser and navigate to both the regular VMware vSphere Compatibility Guide at `http://www.vmware.com/resources/compatibility/search.php` and the VMware VSAN Compatibility Guide at `http://www.vmware.com/resources/compatibility/search.php?deviceCategory=vsan`.

The first link will take you to the standard VMware Compatibility Guide, and the second will take you to the VSAN sub-guide. By default, you will land on the system/server page, to help you select a server platform.

Selecting a server platform

For VSAN, the only requirement in terms of the server platform is that it needs to appear in the regular VMware Compatibility Guide for vSphere 5.5 or 6.0, as applicable to your deployment. Any compatible/certified server is acceptable for use with VSAN.

Getting ready

You should be on the VMware Compatibility Guide Systems/Server page.

How to do it...

You will need to filter your selection to restrict output to only the relevant results. To do this, carry out the following steps:

1. Within **Product Release Version:**, select the most recent vSphere **ESXi 5.5** or **ESXi 6.0** update release.

2. If you have a brand preference, select it within **Partner Name**.

3. While most systems in the Compatibility Guide are rack mount systems, if you have other form-factor needs, select those within **System Type**.

4. If you need dedicated or expanded functionality (such as graphics acceleration for VMware Horizon View or I/O redirection), make that selection within **Features**.

5. Select your CPU socket/core and/or brand needs within the **Sockets:**, **Max Cores per Socket:**, and **CPU Series** sections.

6. VSAN requires at least two CPU cores across one or more sockets. Any field left blank assumes an inclusive search and all subcategories will be included.

7. Once you have selected all of your requirements, click on **Update and View Results** to see a list of all the compatible systems meeting your criteria.

Example of the compatibility guide once filters are applied:

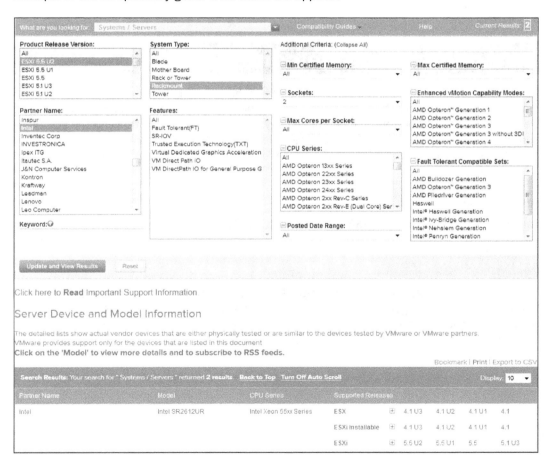

There's more...

VSAN does also impose additional resource needs. Depending on the size of the disks you choose and how many, VSAN will consume additional compute and memory resources. If you typically run your systems close to the margins, in terms of compute/memory resources (or if you are planning to with your new cluster), consider specifying a modest amount of additional CPU and memory in the configuration. VSAN is capped at 10 percent resource utilization for CPU and memory as a maximum, so adding at least 10 percent to your assumed consumption should leave you with comfortable operating margins.

Additionally, VSAN requires a local boot device, either an SD card, or other low-performance solid-state memory, or a dedicated hard disk drive, or SSD. The boot device should be at least 16GB, in accordance with standard VMware recommendations. If your server configuration equals/exceeds 512 GB of system RAM, then you must use a hard disk drive or SSD as your boot device to ensure supportability, otherwise, a core dump cannot be written in the event of a system crash.

Selecting a storage controller

Selecting an appropriate storage controller is one of the most important decisions you will make when creating a VSAN server configuration. The storage controller has tremendous weight in terms of I/O performance and reliability. Because of the importance of the storage controller on the overall performance and reliability of your VSAN cluster the storage controller must be selected from the VSAN-specific subset of the overall VMware Compatibility Guide.

Getting ready

You should be on the VMware VSAN Compatibility Guide page.

How to do it...

The initial landing page for the VSAN Compatibility Guide will allow you to browse through VSAN Ready Node configurations. As we will be discussing the case of VSAN Ready Nodes later in this chapter, for now please click the "Build Your Own based on Certified Components" link from the main page of the VSAN Compatibility Guide:

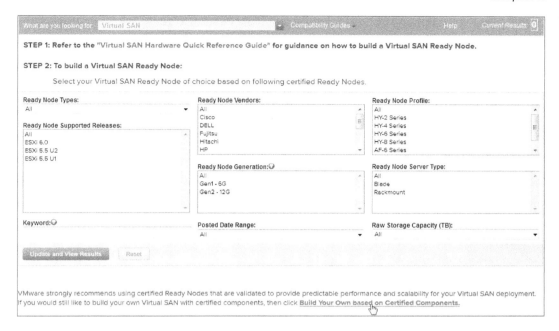

Unlike the regular VMware Compatibility Guide, the VSAN-specific component guide is laid out as a branching tree that you can use to drill down to your desired configuration, after which time hardware choices will be displayed.

1. In the leftmost pane, select **I/O Controller**.

2. In the next pane, select the most-recent vSphere 5.5 or 6.0 update release.

3. In the next pane, select a brand name if desired.

4. In the next pane, specify whether you wish to view the SAS, SAS-RAID, or SAS/SATA RAID controller types.

Some controllers for VSAN support the pass-through (JBOD) mode, and some require you to create single-disk RAID-0 sets. Pass-through controllers tend to be easier to configure and make drive-replacement simpler. RAID-0 controllers are more common and typically have larger queue depths. When selecting controllers and disks, please keep in mind the performance and reliability differences between drive technologies. Generally speaking, SAS and Nearline SAS (NL-SAS) disks have deeper queue depths and are higher-performance. SAS disks are typically more reliable than their SATA and NL-SAS counterparts.

After making your selections, choose **Update and View Results** to get a list of hardware that matches your specifications.

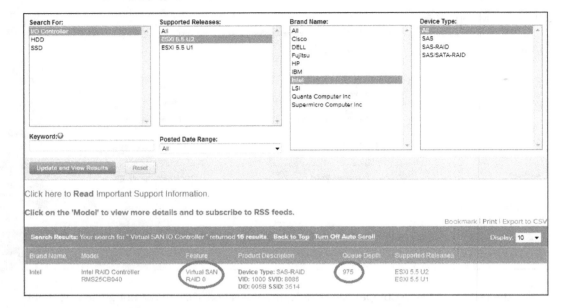

There's more...

Aside from simply ensuring that you select a supported storage controller, the VSAN-specific Compatibility Guide also provides you with additional detail that will be crucial to selecting your storage controller.

This view will tell you whether or not the controller supports the pass-through/JBOD mode and, vitally, it will tell you the controller's command queue depth. The controller's queue depth is a vital consideration. If each node is relatively small with one disk group, any queue depth above 256 commands is acceptable. If you have two disk groups, please consider 512 commands to be the minimum queue depth.

For large or high-performance configurations with several disk groups and extremely large capacities, and/or very high-performance SSDs, you should choose the highest queue depth you can. Standard controllers with maximum queue depths usually have around 1000 commands, like in the preceding example.

Queue depth can have a tremendous effect on the performance of streaming data. Opting for controllers and disks with deeper queues will provide better overall performance, particularly when VSAN is reconfiguring or resynchronizing data.

Selecting a solid-state drive (SSD) for the cache tier

In combination with the storage controller, the SSD for the cache tier is the most important choice you can make in terms of the long-term reliability and performance of your VSAN deployment. The cache-tier SSD is used for caching reads and writes in VSAN hybrid configurations, and for caching writes only in all-flash configurations. SSDs are graded in many ways, and these grades for performance, write resiliency, and fabrication technology will all affect your selection. The VSAN Compatibility Guide gives you an overview of all of these factors to help you make the best choice.

For the SSD:

> ► The write-performance class is on a scale of A-F, with the F class being the fastest (class *A* is technically deprecated).

> ► Write-resiliency is on a scale of A-D, with D being the most resilient.

> ► Fabrication technology is either **multi-layer cell** (**MLC**), or **single-layer cell** (**SLC**). SLC is usually more performant and resilient, at the cost of lower capacities and higher price.

SSDs come in either SATA, SAS, or PCIe connections. PCIe SSD cards are usually at the top end in terms of performance. Given that SAS and PCIe interfaces permit significantly higher device command queues, it is a good idea to use SAS or PCIe type SSDs, especially if you are using a pass-through/JBOD controller that directly leverages device-level command queues.

Getting ready

You should be on the VMware VSAN Compatibility Guide component page.

How to do it...

The Compatibility Guide for SSD is navigated in the same way as for the I/O controller.

1. In the leftmost pane, select **SSD**.
2. In the next pane, select the most recent vSphere 5.5 or 6.0 update release.
3. In the next pane, select a brand name if desired.
4. Specify whether are searching for All Flash or Hybrid cache tier.
5. In the various other fields and drop-down menus, you can select the interface type, manufacturer, performance class, capacity, and form-factor.

6. After making your selections, choose **Update and View Results** to get a list of hardware that matches your specifications:

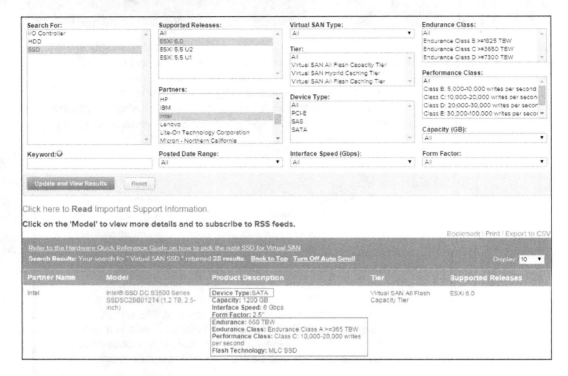

There's more...

Determining the size of your capacity-tier (magnetic or SSD) storage will directly affect the sizing decision for your cache-tier SSD. In general, the SSD should be 10 percent of the size of the magnetic disks in the underlying disk group, for example, if your disk group will consist of four 1.5 TB capacity-tier disks, you will have 6 TB of bulk storage. To accommodate this, the SSD should be about 600 GB. Alternatively, you may choose to opt for two disk groups consisting of three 1TB capacity disks each. In this case, each disk group should have a cache-tier SSD of 300GB. The ratio of cache-tier SSD to capacity-tier disks or SSDs should be approximately 1:10.

See also

For additional guidance regarding how to appropriately size the VSAN capacity and cache tiers, please see the section *Chapter 1 – VSAN Capacity Planning* of *Appendix A, Chapter-specific Expansions*.

Selecting capacity tier disks

The magnetic disks or SSDs you choose will be used for storage capacity and persistent data that is destaged from cache. This is the capacity tier within VSAN, whereas the caching tier SSD will act as the performance caching layer.

In general, you will want to select magnetic disks or SSDs that have adequate capacity to fit your needs. For highly dynamic workloads where data will be frequently destaged from the SSD write buffer and fetched into the SSD read cache, HDD performance is important and you may wish to go with faster disks and/or SAS disks. Only SAS and SATA disks are supported for use with VSAN.

Getting ready

You should be on the VMware VSAN Compatibility Guide component page.

How to do it...

The Compatibility Guide for SSD is navigated in the same way as for the I/O controller

1. In the leftmost pane, select **HDD** or **SSD**.
2. In the next pane, select the most recent vSphere 5.5 or 6.0 update release.
3. In the next pane, select a brand name if desired.
4. In the various other fields and drop-down menus, you can select the interface type, manufacturer, disk speed (RPM), capacity, and form-factor.
   - If we are pursuing an all-flash VSAN configuration, ensure that we select **Virtual SAN All Flash Capacity Tier** from the **Tier:** pane.

5. After making your selections, choose **Update and View Results** to get a list of hardware that matches your specifications.

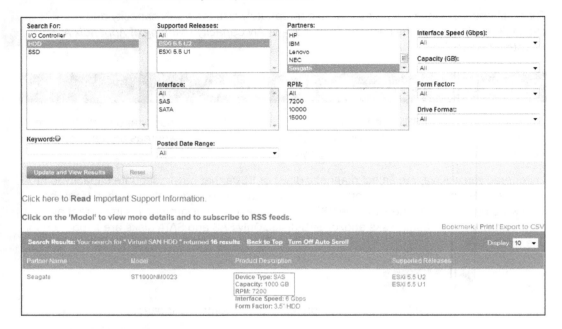

There's more...

In general, SAS disks outperform SATA disks of equivalent capacities and/or rotational speeds because SAS drives use more robust recording technique, deeper queues or both. When cost is a concern, slower SAS drives (typically 7200 RPM; also called near-line SAS or NL-SAS) are usually built on cheaper SATA platforms but include enterprise-grade features like deeper command queues, error-correction, dual-channel connections and native SCSI support. Low-end SAS drives are typically better than high-end SATA drives despite the shared technology platform and costs are usually not significantly higher. NL-SAS is a great alternative to SATA for building out a cost-conscious capacity tier when HDD performance is a factor.

See also

Before settling on a Cache + Capacity disk combination, please review the *Chapter 1 – VSAN Capacity Planning* section of *Appendix A, Chapter-specific Expansions* for a verbose description of the capacity expectations and recommended maximums to help you build your VSAN cluster to an appropriate scale.

Deciding on a network standard

For smaller clusters, network speed is typically only a forefront concern during times of data reconstruction in the event of a node/disk failure, rebalancing, or user-invoked configuration changes. These are generally fairly rare operations and, for the most part, 1GbE networking will be adequate for clusters with fewer than 5 nodes. 10GbE networking is recommended as a VMware best practice for all clusters. 10GbE networking should be considered mandatory for larger clusters, especially clusters of >8 nodes. If 1GbE network interfaces are being used for VSAN, those interfaces need to be dedicated to use by VSAN. 10GbE interfaces can be shared between VSAN and other workloads.

[Unlike disks and storage controllers, there is no special compatibility guide for network controllers. Any vSphere-compatible network controller is acceptable for use with VSAN.]

Getting ready

You should be on the VMware Compatibility Guide IO Devices page.

How to do it...

1. Within **Product Release Version:**, select the most recent vSphere 5.5 or 6.0 update release.
2. If you have a brand preference, select it within **Brand Name**.
3. Select **Network**, within **I/O Device Type**.

4. After making your selections, choose **Update and View Results** to get a list of hardware that matches your specifications.

See also

Before settling on a networking standard, please take a look at a detailed description of the VSAN networking options and recommendations in the VSAN Network Considerations section of *Appendix B, Additional VSAN Information*.

Choosing a VSAN Ready Node (an alternative option)

To help simplify the hardware selection process, numerous VMware partners have preconfigured "VSAN Ready Nodes" that are compliant with the various aspects of the vSphere and VSAN compatibility guides. With VSAN Ready Nodes, the sizing decisions, disk/SSD technology, network standards, and so on, have already been determined by the systems vendor. You may find that a VSAN Ready Node will simplify your purchasing and designing decisions for new VSAN build-outs and/or if you have a preferred system vendor.

Getting ready

You should be on the VMware VSAN Compatibility Guide landing page.

How to do it...

VSAN Ready Nodes are configured by the manufacturer and are designed to target specific infrastructure scales, or for specific use cases, such as **virtual desktops** (**VDI**). These scales are known as **Ready Node Profiles**.

A matrix that defines these profiles can be found by clicking on the **Virtual SAN Hardware Quick Reference Guide** link at the top of the VSAN Compatibility Guide page.

1. The VSAN Compatibility Guide for VSAN Ready Nodes is navigated in a similar manner to the component-oriented Compatibility Guide. The guide is presented as a series of drill-down categories.

2. Select the parameters that fit your needs from the Ready Node type (All Flash or Hybrid), preferred manufacturer, performance/scale profile, form-factor, etc.

3. Once your choices have been selected, click the "Update and View Results" button to populate a list of compliant ready-node configurations:

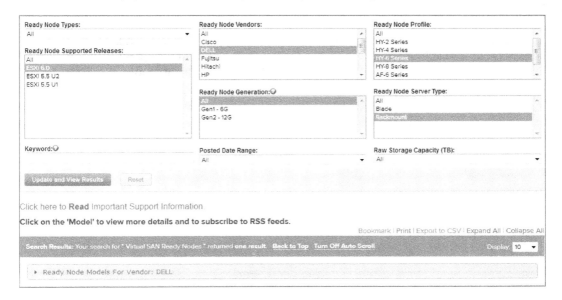

4. The initial output will be a collapsed list of the various Ready Node configurations that are compliant with your selected filters. The output is initially grouped by vendor.

5. To get additional information about the specific Ready Node configuration, twirl down the arrow next to the vendor that you wish to use and then you can expand configuration information about the specific server platform that is recommended:

6. You can then use the SKU number (pictured above) when you contact your preferred vendor to get pricing and ordering information for the Ready Node.

See also

As with user-specified build-outs, please review the *Chapter 1 – VSAN Capacity Planning* section of *Appendix A, Chapter-specific Expansions* for a verbose description of the capacity expectations and recommended maximums, to help you select an appropriate VSAN Ready Node.

2

Initial Configuration and Validation of Your VSAN Cluster

In this chapter, we will discuss the following topics, with a recipe for each:

- ▶ Preparing the vCenter cluster for VSAN
- ▶ Applying VSAN licensing (optional)
- ▶ Configuring VSAN networking on a new standard switch
- ▶ Configuring VSAN networking on an existing switch
- ▶ Enabling SSH on the ESXi hosts (if applicable)
- ▶ Tagging disks as local solid-state drives (if applicable)
- ▶ Enabling VSAN on your cluster
- ▶ Manually claiming disks for use by VSAN (if applicable)
- ▶ Performing initial validation of the new VSAN cluster
- ▶ Enabling vSphere HA

Introduction

In this chapter, you will learn how to pull together all of the bits that you have prepared into a functional VSAN cluster.

By now, you will have selected the appropriate hardware to suit your needs by referencing the VMware Compatibility Guide. You will also have physically deployed your hardware, installed ESXi, created a cluster in vCenter, and added the hosts to that cluster.

Preparing the vCenter cluster for VSAN

There are some cluster-level prerequisites that must be satisfied before VSAN can be enabled. As we have already discussed, you will need a minimum of three hosts, with a minimum of one SSD and one spinning disk or capacity-tier SSD per host. This is probably optional, but it would help with 5.5/6.0 convergence of the text.

In addition, the following prerequisites need to be satisfied:

- Disable vSphere HA
- Apply licensing
- Configure networking
- Tagging disks as SSDs if using RAID-0 mode

Getting ready

You should be logged in to the vSphere Web Client as an administrator or user, authorized to alter cluster-level settings. All VSAN operations must be executed via the vSphere Web Client. The legacy vSphere Client is not supported for VSAN operations.

How to do it...

1. To disable vSphere HA in preparation for VSAN enablement, you must browse the vSphere Web Client. Navigate to **Home** | **Hosts and Clusters** | **Datacenter** | **Cluster** | **Manage**:

2. If vSphere HA is *enabled*, click on the **Edit** button, and then uncheck the **Turn on vSphere HA** checkbox.
3. Click on **OK**, and then monitor the **Recent Tasks** until the process completes.
4. If vSphere HA is not enabled, then no further action is required.

There's more...

Introducing VSAN into a vSphere infrastructure fundamentally changes how vSphere HA works. To permit these changes, vSphere HA must be completely disabled so that we can re-enable it after VSAN is activated. This permits vSphere HA to be reconfigured with knowledge of the VSAN infrastructure and enable proper interoperability.

This step is not optional—disabling vSphere HA is enforced by the VSAN enablement process.

See also

▸ For much greater detail regarding VSAN and HA interoperability, please see the section *Chapter 2 – HA requirements for VSAN enablement* in *Appendix A, Chapter-specific Expansions*

Applying VSAN licensing (optional)

Although it is integrated with vSphere and exists as a native extension to the ESXi hypervisor, VSAN is a separately licensed product. Like all vSphere products, VSAN will enable without a license for the default 60-day evaluation period. Despite this, it is best to license the VSAN cluster prior to full deployment, so as to avoid potential complications resulting from license expiration.

Getting ready

You should be logged in to the vSphere Web Client as an administrator or user, authorized to alter cluster-level settings and licensing/entitlement.

How to do it...

To add your VSAN license, you must browse the vSphere Web Client:

1. Navigate to **Home | Licensing | License Keys**.
2. Click on the green **+** icon to add a license key.
3. Enter or paste your license key into the textbox.
4. Click on **Next**.

How it works...

VSAN is licensed per-cluster. As VSAN is a distributed product, it is cluster-centric rather than host-centric. The license is applied to the vSphere cluster within vCenter, and the license is consumed by the ESXi hosts/VSAN nodes as applicable per the terms of your license.

 If VSAN is using CPU-based licensing, all hosts in the VSAN cluster, even any nodes *not* contributing storage, will consume VSAN license capacity.

There's more...

There are a variety of licensing options for VSAN, depending on your use case. You can license VSAN specifically for **virtual desktop infrastructure** (**VDI**) using VMware Horizon View, as a service provider or for general-purpose production. Regardless of which license type you use, you apply the license using this recipe.

For more information regarding which license type is best for your needs, please contact your VMware representative or retail partner.

Configuring VSAN networking on a new standard switch

 If you are using the distributed virtual switch or already have a vSwitch configured, please skip this recipe and continue to the next recipe, *Configuring VSAN networking on an existing switch*.

Networking is the glue that holds the VSAN distributed storage nodes together. To permit redundancy, storage access, policy management, and so on, a robust and properly-configured network is key. From within vSphere, VSAN is enabled on a network interface as a service. If you are familiar with creating and enabling vMotion, management, and fault tolerance interfaces, you are already familiar with this process!

This recipe will cover the creation of a new VMkernel network interface in a new vSwitch with previously unused physical network adapters.

Getting ready

▶ You should be logged in to the vSphere Web Client as an administrator or user, authorized to alter cluster-level settings and networking.

▶ There should be physical 1GbE or 10GbE interfaces available for use by VSAN.

▶ VSAN network interfaces should be configured to use a unique IP subnet that is not otherwise in use in the infrastructure. This IP subnet does not need to be routable.

▶ A separate VLAN for VSAN traffic is optional.

▶ Your upstream physical switch should be able to handle multicast traffic on the interfaces used by VSAN.

How to do it...

1. Navigate to **Home** | **Hosts and Clusters** | **Datacenter** | **Cluster** | **Host** | **Manage** | **Networking**:

2. Click on **Add host networking**:

3. Under **Select connection type**, choose **vmkernel**, and then click on **Next**:

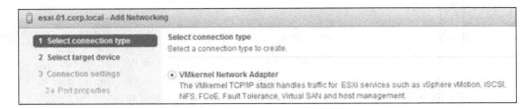

4. Under **Select target device**, choose **New standard switch**, and then click on **Next**:

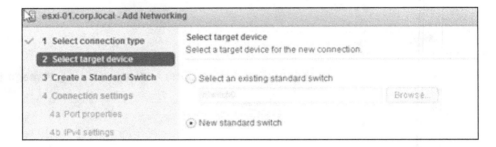

5. When prompted, select the applicable physical network adapters and click on **OK**, and then on **Next**:

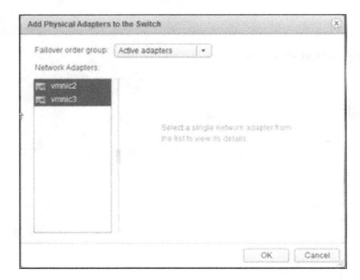

6. Under **Port properties**, enter a label for the new interface, a **VLAN ID** if appropriate, and check the **Virtual SAN traffic** box:

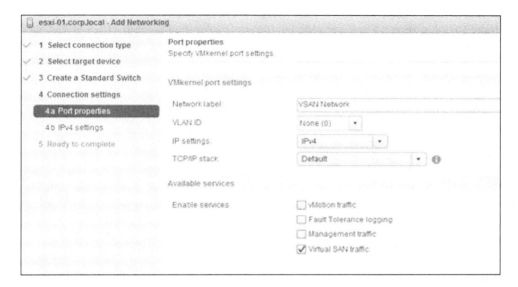

7. Apply your network address. Ideally, the subnet should be unique (not used for management, vMotion, or fault tolerance):

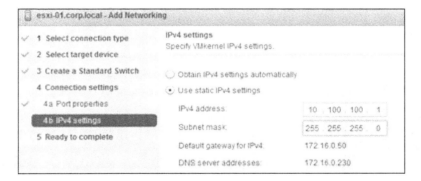

8. Complete the wizard.

9. Finally, complete this recipe on all hosts in the VSAN cluster.

How it works...

As VSAN is a unique service at the hypervisor level, the service is bound to a specific VMkernel interface. This is similar behavior to vMotion and fault tolerance tagging. There is no *best-effort* networking with VSAN. If there are no tagged interfaces, the host will *not* be able to join the VSAN cluster and will be network isolated. Subsequently, HA configuration will also fail.

There's more...

The VSAN network should be in its own unique IP subnet to help avoid potential network irregularities related to default routes (for example, to prevent routed traffic from using VSAN VMkernel network interfaces to access the gateway). While VSAN interfaces can function in existing subnets and traffic will be restricted to the tagged interface, it is the best practice to give it its own subnet for maximum compatibility and reliability across the entire virtual and physical infrastructures.

VSAN traffic can be shared with other VMkernel interfaces, such as those used for vMotion. This is not ideal, however, as service separation across VMkernel interfaces is preferred. There is no harm with sharing VSAN traffic and non-VSAN traffic across physical 10GbE interfaces (for example, the VSAN VMkernel interface can exist in the same vSwitch/uplink set with non-VSAN interfaces). If you are using 1GbE physical interfaces, those interfaces should be dedicated to VSAN per VMware best practices.

See also

> ▸ For more information about physical networking requirements, multicast, LACP/link-aggregation, and so on, please see the *Appendix B, Additional VSAN Information* specifically, if desired.

Configuring VSAN networking on an existing switch

 If you need to create a new standard switch for VSAN traffic, please skip this recipe and go back to the previous recipe, *Configuring VSAN networking on a new standard switch*.

Networking is the glue that holds the VSAN distributed storage nodes together. To permit redundancy, storage delivery, policy management, and so on, a robust and properly-configured network is key. From within vSphere, VSAN is enabled on a network interface as a service. If you are familiar with creating and enabling vMotion, management, and fault tolerance interfaces, you are already familiar with this process!

This recipe will cover the creation of a new VMkernel network interface in an existing vSwitch or dvPortGroup.

Getting ready

- ▶ You should be logged in to the vSphere Web Client as an administrator or user, authorized to alter cluster-level settings and networking
- ▶ There should be physical 1GbE or 10GbE interfaces available for use by VSAN
- ▶ You should have a unique IP subnet available for application to VSAN interfaces
- ▶ A separate VLAN for VSAN traffic is optional
- ▶ Your upstream physical switch should be able to handle multicast traffic on the interfaces used by VSAN

How to do it...

1. Navigate to **Home | Hosts and Clusters | Datacenter | Cluster | Host | Manage | Networking**:

2. Click on **Add host networking**:

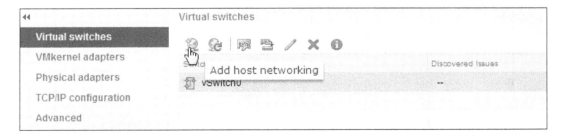

3. Under **Select connection type**, choose **vmkernel**, and then click on **Next**:

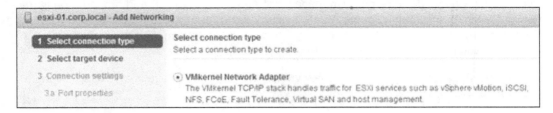

4. Under **Select target device**, choose your existing vSwitch or distributed port group, and then click on **Next**. This example uses a dvPortGroup called **VSAN**:

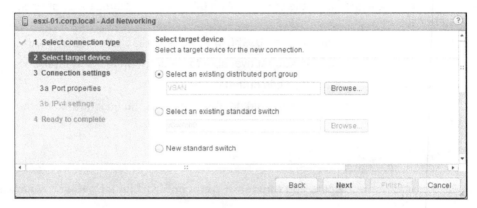

5. Under **Port properties**, enter a network label (if applicable), and then check the **Virtual SAN traffic** checkbox, and then on click **Next**:

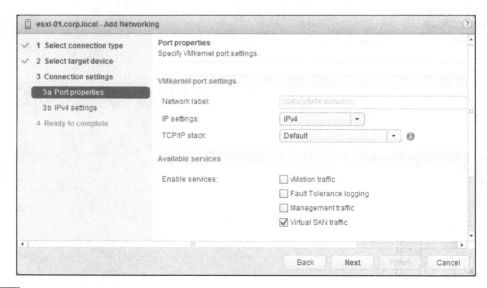

6. Under **IPv4 settings**, assign an address in a subnet unique to VSAN, or choose automatic configuration if you use DHCP. Then, click on **Next**:

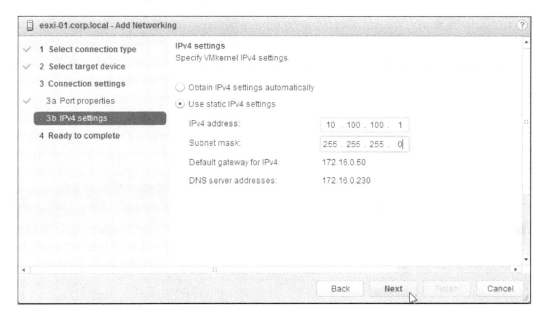

7. Finish the wizard.
8. Complete this recipe on all hosts in the VSAN cluster.

How it works...

As VSAN is a unique service at the hypervisor level, the service is bound to a specific VMkernel interface. This is similar behavior to vMotion and fault tolerance tagging. There is no *best-effort* networking with VSAN. If there are no tagged interfaces, the host will *not* be able to join the VSAN cluster and will be network-isolated. Subsequently, HA configuration will also fail.

There's more...

The VSAN network should be in its own unique IP subnet to help avoid potential network irregularities related to default routes (for example, to prevent routed traffic from using VSAN VMkernel network interfaces to access the gateway). While VSAN interfaces can function in existing subnets, and traffic will be restricted to the tagged interface, it is the best practice to give it its own subnet for maximum compatibility and reliability across the entire virtual and physical infrastructures.

VSAN traffic can be shared with other VMkernel interfaces, such as those used for vMotion. This is not ideal, however, as service separation across VMkernel interfaces is preferred. There is no harm with sharing VSAN traffic and non-VSAN traffic across physical 10GbE interfaces (for example, the VSAN VMkernel interface can exist in the same vSwitch/uplink set with non-VSAN interfaces). If you are using 1GbE physical interfaces, those interfaces should be dedicated to VSAN as per VMware best practices.

See also

> ► For more information about physical networking requirements, multicast, LACP/link-aggregation, and so on, please see the *Appendix B, Additional VSAN Information* specifically, if desired.

Enabling SSH on the ESXi hosts (if applicable)

 If you are running vSphere 6.0, please skip this section and refer to the *Tagging disks as SSDs in vSphere 6.0* recipe in *Chapter 9, VSAN 6.0*, if you need to tag your disks as SSDs.

If you need to tag disks as SSD devices, you will need CLI access to the ESXi host. If we are using RAID-0 storage controllers, ESXi will detect the SSDs as normal magnetic drives due to the way RAID-0 controllers present storage to the operating system. The tagging process will only be applicable to SSDs that were not correctly identified as such by default. The SSD-tagging process requires several commands in vSphere 5.5 and it is easiest to perform these steps via a remote console (SSH).

 If SSH is already enabled on your hosts or if you will not need to tag SSDs, please skip this recipe.

Getting ready

You should be logged in to the vSphere Web Client as an administrator or user, authorized to alter host-level security profile settings.

How to do it...

To enable SSH, you must browse the vSphere Web Client.

1. Navigate to **Home** | **Hosts and Clusters** | **Datacenter** | **Host** | **Manage** | **Settings** | **Security Profile**. Scroll down to **Services** and click on **Edit...**:

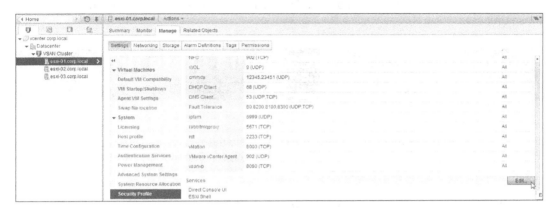

2. Select **SSH** from the list, and then click on **Start**:

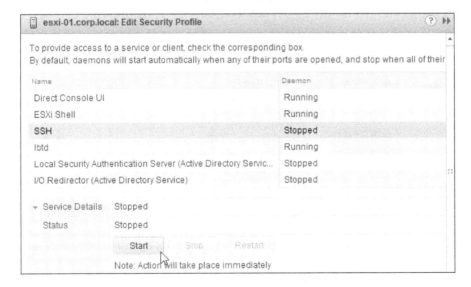

3. Once the service starts, click on **OK**.
4. Complete this recipe on all hosts in the VSAN cluster.

How it works...

Once followed, this recipe will enable SSH access on all hosts. This will enable you to log in to the ESXi host remotely using an SSH terminal emulator. The changes made here will persist until you turn SSH off or until you reboot your ESXi host.

If you have previously enabled SSH or ESXi Shell service timeouts, you will be constrained by those timeouts.

Tagging disks as local solid-state drives (if applicable)

If you are running vSphere 6.0, please skip this section and refer to the *Tagging disks as SSDs in vSphere 6.0* recipe in *Chapter 9, VSAN 6.0*, if you need to tag your disks as SSDs.

Depending on the type of storage controller you are using, you may need to tell ESXi which disks are your solid-state drives. If your storage controllers present disks to the ESXi as a RAID-0 device, you will need to follow this recipe to inform ESXi about which disks are your SSDs. This recipe must be followed if devices that you know to be SSDs are detected as non-SSDs.

If your storage controllers present disks to the ESXi host in pass-through mode, you may skip this recipe as the ESXi storage stack would automatically detect the SSD devices.

Getting ready

- ▶ You should have enabled SSH on your ESXi hosts that are used for VSAN (see previous recipe)
- ▶ You should know the size/capacity of your SSD device(s) so that they can be identified and tagged
- ▶ You should be logged in to the vSphere Web Client as an administrator or user, authorized to view host storage settings
- ▶ You should know your ESXi host root password(s)

How to do it...

1. In the vSphere Web Client, navigate to: **Home | Hosts and Clusters | Datacenter | Cluster | Host | Manage | Storage | Storage Devices**:

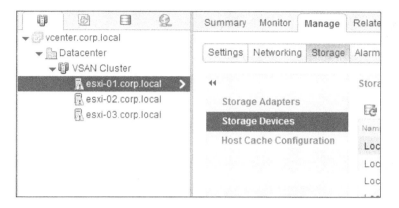

2. Find your SSD device in the list and highlight it. In this case, the SSD is the **17.00 GB** device:

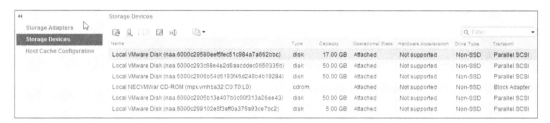

3. In the lower pane, highlight and copy the identifier to the clipboard.

4. This will usually begin with `naa.`, but depending on your storage controller type, it could also begin with `mpx.`, `t10.`, or `eui`.

5. Log in to the ESXi host via SSH as the root user.

6. Get disk information about the device. You should see information about the device, including `Is SSD: false`. The command to run is:

```
# esxcli storage core device list -d <disk identifier>
```

For example:

```
# esxcli storage core device list -d naa.6000c29580eef5fec51c984a7
a662bbc
naa.6000c29580eef5fec51c984a7a662bbc
    Display Name: Local VMware Disk (naa.6000c29580eef5fec51c984a7a
662bbc)
    Has Settable Display Name: true
    Size: 17408
    Device Type: Direct-Access
    Multipath Plugin: NMP
Devfs Path: /vmfs/devices/disks/naa.6000c29580eef5fec51c984a7a662b
bc
    Vendor: VMware
    Model: Virtual disk
    Revision: 1.0
    SCSI Level: 2
    Is Pseudo: false
    Status: on
    Is RDM Capable: false
    Is Local: true
    Is Removable: false
Is SSD: false
```

7. Write an SATP claim rule to identify the disk as an SSD. The command to run this is:

```
# esxcli storage nmpsatp rule add --satp=VMW_SATP_LOCAL --device
<disk identifier> --option "enable_ssd"
```

> If the `esxcli storage core device list` output indicates
> `Is Local: false`, then you will also need to tag the disk as a local
> device. If you need to perform this step, the command is:
>
> ```
> # esxcli storage nmpsatp rule add --satp=VMW_SATP_
> LOCAL --device <disk identifier> --option "enable_ssd
> enable_local"
> ```

For example:

```
# esxcli storage nmpsatp rule add --satp=VMW_SATP_LOCAL --device
naa.6000c29580eef5fec51c984a7a662bbc --option "enable_ssd"
```

8. Load your new claim rule and execute it:

```
# esxcli storage core claimrule load
# esxcli storage core claimrule run
```

9. Unclaim your SSD device. This will permit it to be rediscovered as an SSD. The command to do this is:

```
# esxcli storage core claiming unclaim --type=device --device
<disk identifier>
```

For example:

```
# esxcli storage core claiming unclaim --type=device --device naa.
6000c29580eef5fec51c984a7a662bbc
```

10. Rescan your storage adapters:

```
# esxcli storage core adapter rescan --all
```

11. Reclaim the storage device using the new rules. The command to do this is:

```
# esxcli storage core claiming reclaim --device <disk identifier>
```

For example:

```
# esxcli storage core claiming reclaim --device naa.6000c29580eef5
fec51c984a7a662bbc
```

12. Rerun the `esxcli storage core device list -d <disk identifier>` command as in step 5. You should find that the disk now reads `Is SSD: true` and `Is Local: true`.

13. Complete this recipe on all the hosts in the VSAN cluster.

How it works...

The reason this step is necessary relates to VSAN requirements in the context of how storage controllers present devices to the hypervisor's storage stack. VSAN requires an SSD device, and validates that the device is an SSD by reading the device inquiry data.

With pass-through devices (raw disks), this is easily achieved as the SSD will identify itself as such during standard SCSI inquiry. On non-pass-through (RAID-0) devices, however, this is not the case and the RAID device will not provide any SSD-related information during a standard SCSI inquiry. When using RAID-0 mode, ESXi is not being given a disk as such—it is being given a logical RAID device provisioned by the storage controller. The fact that there is only one disk in that RAID set and that the one disk is an SSD is unfortunately immaterial. The storage controller presents a device to the ESXi host using its own presentation rules, and that does not include SSD information on any controller currently certified for use with VSAN.

Because of this, we must manually override the default settings obtained through the SCSI inquiry. The process outlined in this recipe does exactly that. We identify the device that we, as administrators, know to be the SSD. We then write a custom rule to instruct ESXi to override the information obtained via the SCSI inquiry with our pre-defined information. This allows ESXi to identify the device as a local SSD. In turn, this will allow the VSAN processes to identify the SSD and differentiate it from regular spinning disks when we build disk groups later in this chapter.

Enabling VSAN on your cluster

Now that we have prepared the cluster, applied licensing, configured networking, and prepared the physical disks, we are finally ready to enable VSAN on the cluster. The hard part is done—from here, the process is very simple and we will have a functional VSAN cluster in just a few more steps!

Getting ready

You should be logged in to the vSphere Web Client as an administrator or user, authorized to alter cluster-level settings and VSAN.

How to do it...

1. From the vSphere Web Client, navigate to: **Home | Hosts and Clusters | Datacenter | Cluster | Manage | Virtual SAN | General**, and click on the **Edit...** button:

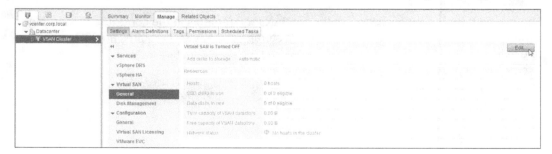

2. Check the **Turn ON Virtual SAN** checkbox and select your disk-claiming rules by selecting the appropriate option from the **Add disks to storage** drop-down menu, and then click on **OK**.

You have two options for disk claiming

Automatic mode will automatically claim all unused disks and SSDs for use by VSAN and will automatically construct your disk groups. When in **Automatic** mode, manual overrides and configuration changes (decommissioning disk groups, selective expansion of disk groups, and so on) are not possible.

Manual mode will enable VSAN but will not claim any disks for you or build any disk groups. If you choose this option, you must manually claim disks.

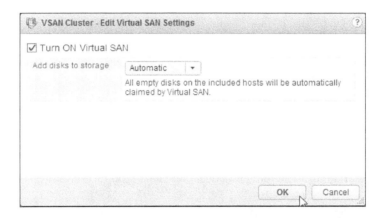

3. VSAN will then be enabled, and if applicable, disk groups will be automatically created. This process can take some time. Please monitor the task progress in the **Recent Tasks** pane in the vSphere Web Client.

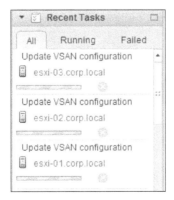

How it works...

After checking the **Turn ON Virtual SAN** box, vCenter will coordinate cluster creation amongst all hosts in the cluster. The cluster will be formed and all hosts will join following an election. If you opted for automatic disk claiming, the disks will be partitioned and the disk group relationships (spinning disks and SSDs) built.

If you opted for automatic claiming, the cluster will now be formed and storage will be available and ready to use.

There's more...

Automatic disk-claiming mode can potentially preclude certain operations in the future.

In automatic mode, disks are managed in a *totally* automated way, with no possibility of manual overrides. If you wish to destroy a disk group in the future, you will be unable to do so if the cluster is set to automatic mode for disk claiming. To perform certain maintenance tasks like decommissioning a group, you will need to move the cluster into **Manual** mode from the VSAN general settings page. You can reach that field by repeating steps one and two in this recipe.

See also

> ▸ For the manual disk claiming process, please see the next recipe

Manually claiming disks for use by VSAN (if applicable)

If you opted for manual disk claiming, VSAN will be enabled but the datastore will have no capacity. We will add capacity by manually determining which disks should be used by Virtual SAN.

[If you are using automatic disk claiming, please skip this recipe.]

Getting ready

You should be logged in to the vSphere Web Client as an administrator or user, authorized to alter cluster-level settings and VSAN.

How to do it...

1. From the vSphere Web Client, navigate to: **Home | Hosts and Clusters | Datacenter | Cluster | Manage | Virtual SAN | Disk Management** and click on the **Claim disks** button:

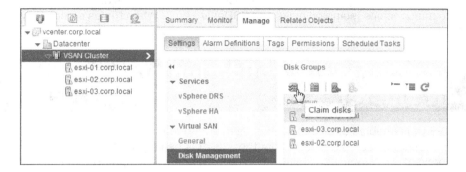

2. In the resulting box, you can select which SSD and spinning disks to claim on a per-host basis. If you want to claim everything, you can click on the **Select all eligible disks** button. Once you have selected the disks you wish to use, click on the **OK** button:

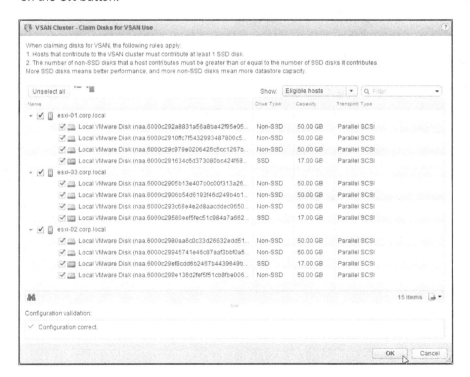

3. Depending on the number of nodes, disks, and disk groups, this process can take some time. Monitor it in the **Recent Tasks** pane in the vSphere Web Client.

How it works...

Based on the parameters you defined during disk claiming, the disks are partitioned and the disk group relationships (spinning disks and SSDs) are built. When that is complete, your VSAN cluster will have available capacity and be able to provision VMs.

Performing initial validation of the new VSAN cluster

Now that VSAN is enabled and capacity has been added to the new cluster, we should perform a few initial validation steps to ensure that the cluster is healthy. Performing these steps now can help prevent provisioning or availability errors later on when we start to create VMs in the new VSAN cluster.

Getting ready

You should be logged in to the vSphere Web Client as an administrator or user, authorized to alter cluster-level settings, VSAN, and VASA providers.

How to do it...

Verify the disk and network groups:

1. From the vSphere Web Client, navigate to: **Home | Hosts and Clusters | Datacenter | Cluster | Manage | Virtual SAN | Disk Management**.

2. Examine the disk-group layout. Assuming that all hosts contribute storage to the VSAN cluster, there should be at least one disk group associated with each host. All hosts should be **Healthy** and show **State** as **Connected**, and all **Network Partition Group** hosts should be **Group 1**:

Verify that the VSAN datastore has capacity:

1. From the vSphere Web Client, navigate to: **Home | Storage | Datacenter | vsanDatastore | Summary**.

2. Examine the **Summary** tab. You should see that the **vsanDatastore** has capacity and low utilization. All hosts in the cluster should be connected to the datastore:

Verify that the VASA providers are registered:

1. From the vSphere Web Client, navigate to: **Home | vCenter | vCenter Servers**. Now, click on the vCenter name, and then navigate to **Manage | Storage Providers**.

2. Examine the registered storage providers. There should be a group for **vsanDatastore**. The group should have the same number of providers as there are hosts in the cluster. One of these will be **Active** and the remainder will be **Standby**:

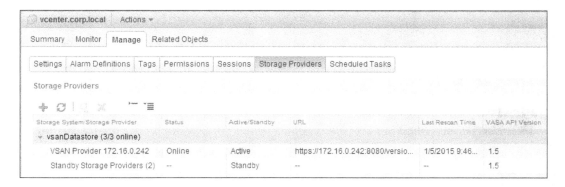

How it works...

This recipe involves a spot-check of the primary aspects of a VSAN cluster that will be present after the cluster is activated. A failure of any of these verifications will warrant additional troubleshooting before proceeding with the following chapters.

There's more...

By default, all hosts will have access to the VSAN datastore and that datastore will have available capacity. All hosts should be able to communicate with each other as well as the vCenter Server.

The storage providers automatically register with the vCenter Server, and these enable the VSAN-specific policy-based management tasks that you will use during day-to-day operations with VSAN.

See also

> ▶ If any of these validation steps fail, please skip ahead to the troubleshooting chapter to resolve those issues prior to proceeding with the next chapters

Enabling vSphere HA

Now that the VSAN cluster is created and validated, we are ready to re-enable vSphere HA. This process is the same as it was prior to the introduction of VSAN.

Getting ready

You should be logged in to the vSphere Web Client as an administrator or user, authorized to alter cluster-level settings.

How to do it...

1. From the vSphere Web Client, navigate to: **Home** | **Hosts and Clusters** | **Datacenter** | **Cluster** | **Manage** | **Services** | **vSphere HA**.

2. Click on the **Edit...** button:

3. In the subsequent menu, check the **Turn ON vSphere HA** checkbox.

4. Select any monitoring, admission control, and **Datastore Heartbeating** options, as per your infrastructure and administrative needs.

5. Click on **OK**:

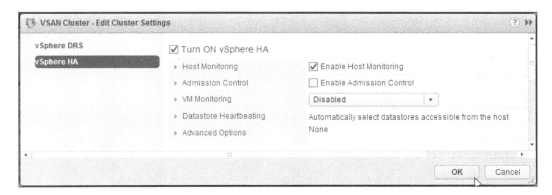

6. This process can take some time. Monitor the progress in the **Recent Tasks** pane and investigate any HA-related failures as needed.

How it works...

Enabling vSphere HA after VSAN has been enabled, permits vSphere HA to be reconfigured with knowledge of the VSAN infrastructure, and enables proper interoperability. This optimizes HA so that it follows the underlying VSAN availability.

See also

▶ For much greater detail on VSAN and HA interoperability, please see the section *Chapter 2 – HA requirements for VSAN enablement* in *Appendix A, Chapter-specific Expansions*

3
Storage Policy-based Management

In this chapter, we will discuss the following topics, with a recipe for each:

- Creating VM storage policies
- Applying storage policies to a new VM or a VM deployed from a template
- Applying storage policies to an existing VM migrating to VSAN
- Viewing a VM's storage policies and object distribution
- Changing storage policies on a VM already residing in VSAN
- Modifying existing storage policies

Introduction

Now that we have a functional VSAN cluster, we can leverage the power of **Storage Policy-based Management** (**SPBM**) to control how we deploy our **virtual machines** (**VMs**). SPBM is where the administrative power of converged infrastructure becomes apparent. You can define VM-thick provisioning on a sliding scale, define how fault tolerant the VM's storage should be, make distribution and performance decisions, and more. RAID-type decisions for VMs resident on VSAN are also driven through the use of SPBM. VSAN can provide RAID-1 (mirrored) and RAID-0 (striped) configurations, or a combination of the two in the form of RAID-10 (mirrored set of stripes).

All of this is done on a per-VM basis. As the storage and compute infrastructures are now converged, you can define how you want a VM to run in the most logical place—at the VM level or its disks. The need for a datastore-centric configuration, storage tiering, and so on is obviated and made redundant through the power of SPBM.

Technically, the configuration of storage policies is optional. If you choose not to define any storage policies, VSAN will create VMs and disks according to its default cluster-wide storage policy. While this will provide for generic levels of fault tolerance and performance, it is *strongly recommended* to create and apply storage policies according to your administrative need. Much of the power given to you through a converged infrastructure and VSAN is in the policy-driven and VM-centric nature of policy-based management.

 All storage policy definitions provided by VSAN are discussed in the *Chapter 3A – VSAN-specifi storage-policy options* section of *Appendix A, Chapter-specific Expansions*. While some of these options will be discussed throughout the following recipes, it is strongly recommended that you review the storage-policy appendix to familiarize yourself with all the storage-policy options prior to continuing.

Creating VM storage policies

Before a storage policy can be applied, it must be created. Once created, the storage policy can be applied to any part of any VM resident on VSAN-connected storage. You will probably want to create a number of storage policies to suit your production needs. Once created, all storage policies are tracked by vCenter and enforced/maintained by VSAN itself. Because of this, your policy selections remain valid and production continues even in the event of a vCenter outage.

 In the example policy that we will create in this recipe, the VM policy will be defined as tolerating the failure of a single VSAN host. The VM will not be required to stripe across multiple disks and it will be 30% thick-provisioned.

Getting ready

Your VSAN should be deployed and functional as per the previous chapter. You should be logged in to the vSphere Web Client as an administrator or as a user with rights to create, modify, apply, and delete storage policies.

How to do it...

1. From the vSphere 5.5 Web Client, navigate to **Home | VM Storage Policies**.

2. From the vSphere 6.0 Web Client, navigate to **Home | Policies and Profiles | VM Storage Policies**. Initially, there will be no storage policies defined unless you have already created storage policies for other solutions. This is normal.

 In VSAN 6.0, you will have the VSAN default policy defined here prior to the creation of your own policies.

3. Click the **Create a new VM storage policy** button:

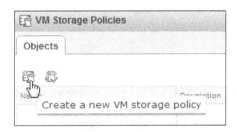

4. A wizard will launch to guide you through the process.

5. If you have multiple vCenter Server systems in linked-mode, ensure that you have selected the appropriate vCenter Server system from the drop-down menu.

6. Give your storage policy a name that will be useful to you and a description of what the policy does. Then, click **Next**:

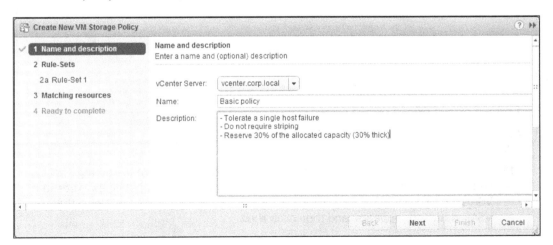

7. The next page describes the concept of rule sets and requires no interaction. Click the **Next** button to proceed.

8. When creating the rule set, ensure that you select **VSAN** from the **Rules based on vendor-specific capabilities** drop-down menu. This will expose the **<Add capability>** button. Select **Number of failures to tolerate** from the drop-down menu and specify a value of 1:

9. Add other capabilities as desired. For this example, we will specify a single stripe with 30% space reservation.

10. Once all required policy definitions have been applied, click **Next**:

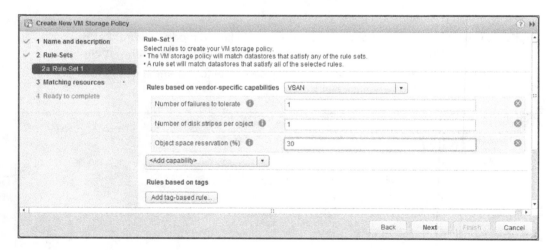

11. The next page will tell you which datastores are compatible with the storage policy you have created. As this storage policy is based on specific capabilities exposed by VSAN, only your VSAN datastore will appear as a matching resource. Verify that the VSAN datastore appears, and then click **Next**.

12. Review the summary page and ensure that the policy is being created on the basis of your specifications. When finished, click **Finish**.

13. The policy will be created. Depending on the speed of your system, this operation should be nearly instantaneous but may take several seconds to finish.

How it works...

The VSAN-specific policy definitions are presented through VMware Profile-Driven Storage service, which runs with vCenter Server. Profile-Driven Storage Service determines which policy definitions are available by communicating with the ESXi hosts that are enabled for VSAN. Once VSAN is enabled, each host activates a VASA provider daemon, which is responsible for communicating policy options to and receiving policy instructions from Profile-Driven Storage Service.

There's more...

The nature of the storage policy definitions enabled by VSAN is additive. No policy option mutually excludes any other, and they can be combined in any way that your policy requirements demand. For example, specifying a number of failures to tolerate will not preclude the specification cache reservation.

See also

▸ For a full explanation of all policy options and when you might want to use them, please see the *Chapter 3A – VSAN-specific storage-policy options* section of *Appendix A, Chapter-specific Expansions*

Applying storage policies to a new VM or a VM deployed from a template

When creating a new VM on VSAN, you will want to apply a storage policy to that VM according to your administrative needs. As VSAN is fully integrated into vSphere and vCenter, this is a straightforward option during the normal VM deployment wizard.

> The workflow described in this recipe is for creating a new VM on VSAN. If deployed from a template, the wizard process is functionally identical from step 4 of the *How to do it...* section in this recipe.

Getting ready

You should be logged into vSphere Web Client as an administrator or a user authorized to create virtual machines.

You should have at least one storage policy defined (see previous recipe).

How to do it...

1. Navigate to **Home** | **Hosts and Clusters** | **Datacenter** | **Cluster**.
2. Right-click the cluster, and then select **New Virtual Machine...**:

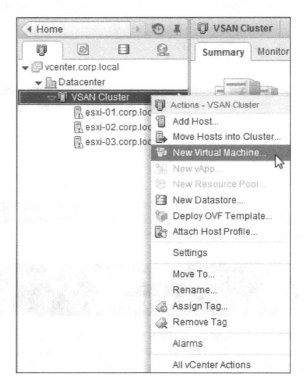

3. In the subsequent screen, select **Create a new virtual machine**.
4. Proceed through the wizard through Step **2b**. For the compute resource, ensure that you select your VSAN cluster or one of its hosts:

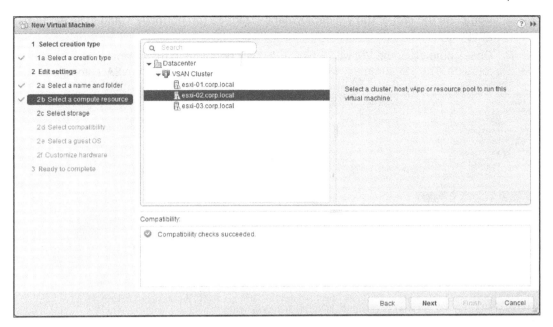

5. On the next step, select one of the VM storage policies that you created in the previous recipe. Once you select a VSAN storage policy, only the VSAN datastore will appear as compatible. Any other datastores that you have present will be ineligible for selection:

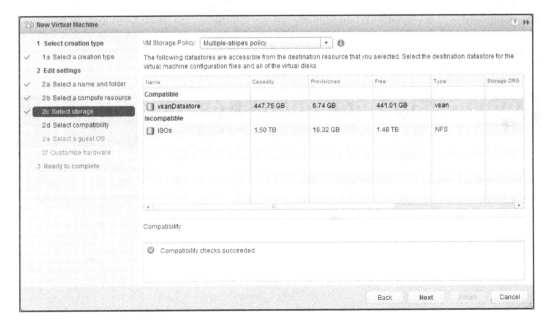

6. Complete the rest of the VM-deployment wizard as you normally would to select the guest OS, resources, and so on.

7. Once completed, the VM will deploy and it will populate in the inventory tree on the left side. The VM summary will reflect that the VM resides on the VSAN storage:

How it works...

All VMs resident on the VSAN storage will have a storage policy applied. Selecting the appropriate policy during VM creation means that the VM will be how you want it to be from the beginning of the VM's life. While policies can be changed later, this could involve a reconfiguration of the object, which can take time to complete and can result in increased disk and network traffic once it is initiated. Careful decision making during deployment can help you save time later.

Applying storage policies to an existing VM migrating to VSAN

When introducing VSAN into an existing infrastructure, you may have existing VMs that reside on the external storage, such as NFS, iSCSI, or **Fibre Channel** (**FC**). When the time comes to move these VMs into your converged infrastructure and VSAN, we will have to make policy decisions about how these VMs should be handled.

Getting ready

You should be logged into vSphere Web Client as an administrator or a user authorized to create, migrate, and modify VMs.

How to do it...

1. Navigate to **Home** | **Hosts and Clusters** | **Datacenter** | **Cluster**.

2. Identify the VM that you wish to migrate to VSAN. For the example used in this recipe, we will migrate the VM called **linux-vm02** that resides on **NFS Datastore**.

3. Right-click the VM and select **Migrate...** from the context menu:

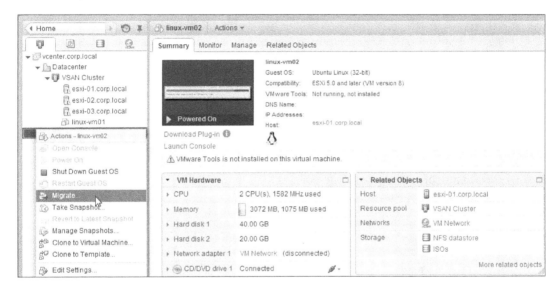

4. In the resulting page, select **Change datastore** or **Change both host and datastore** as applicable, and then click **Next**.

 If the VM does not already reside on one of your VSAN-enabled hosts, you must choose the **Change both host and datastore** option for your migration.

5. In the next step, select one of the VM storage policies that you created in the previous recipe. Once you select a VSAN storage policy, only the VSAN datastore will appear as compatible. Any other datastores that you have present will be ineligible for selection:

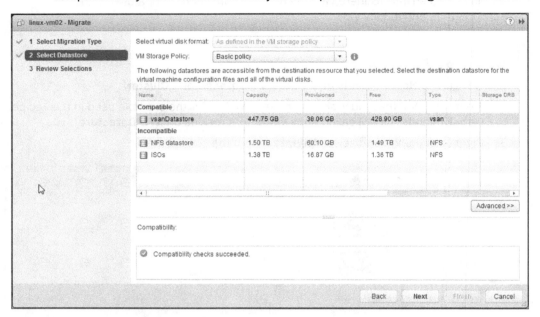

You can apply different storage policies to different VM disks. This can be done by performing the following steps:

1. Click on the **Advanced >>** button to reveal various parts of the VM:

 Once clicked, the **Advanced >>** button will change to **<< Basic**.

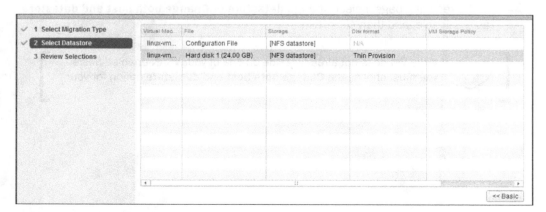

2. In the **Storage** column, click the existing datastore to reveal a drop-down menu. Click **Browse**. In the subsequent window, select the desired policy from the **VM Storage Policy** drop-down menu. You will find that the only compatible datastore is your VSAN datastore. Click **OK**:

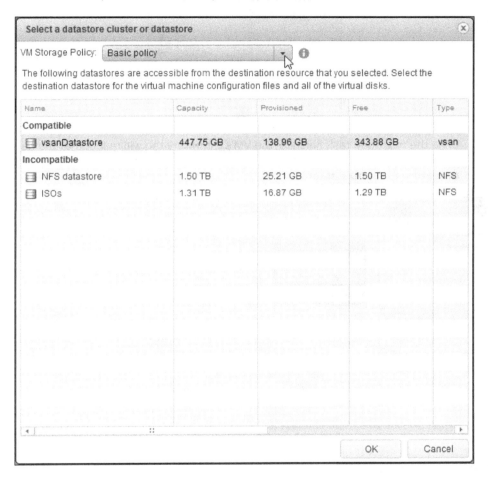

3. Repeat the preceding step as needed for other disks and the VM configuration file.

6. After performing the preceding steps, click on **Next**.

7. Review your selection on the final page, and then click **Finish**.

8. Migrations can potentially take a long time, depending on how large the VM is, the speed of the network, and other considerations. Please monitor the progress of your VM relocation tasks using the **Recent Tasks** pane:

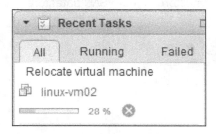

9. Once the migration task finishes, the VM's **Summary** tab will reflect that the datastore is now the VSAN datastore. For the example of this VM, the VM moved from **NFS Datastore** to **vsanDatastore**:

How it works...

Much like the new VM workflow, we select the storage policy that we want to use during the migration of the VM to VSAN. However, unlike the deploy-from-template or VM-creation workflows, this process requires none of the VM configuration steps. We only have to select the storage policy, and then SPBM instructs VSAN how to place and distribute the objects. All object-distribution activities are completely transparent and automatic.

This process can be used to change the storage policy of a VM already resident in the VSAN cluster, but it is more cumbersome than modifying the policies by other means. Please see the *Changing storage policies on a VM already residing in VSAN* recipe for more information.

Viewing a VM's storage policies and object distribution

Once you have multiple VMs in your VSAN cluster, it becomes important to understand how to examine the VMs to determine which policies are applied and whether the VMs comply with these policies.

As your infrastructure grows, it becomes vital to be able to effectively examine and monitor your VMs to ensure that everything is working and distributed as expected.

Getting ready

You should be logged into vSphere Web Client as an administrator or a user permitted to view VM configuration details.

How to do it...

1. In vSphere Web Client, navigate to **Home** | **Hosts and Clusters** | **Datacenter** | **Cluster**.

2. Select the VM that you wish to examine. For this example, we will examine the **linux-vm02** VM that we migrated to VSAN in the previous recipe.

3. On the VM's **Summary** page, you will see the policy that is applied, compliance status, and the last time that vCenter checked this VM for compliance:

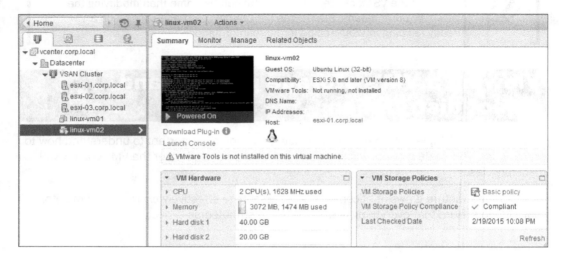

4. This at-a-glance view tells us which policy is applied and whether we are compliant. However, we cannot determine how the VM is distributed throughout the cluster. To examine this information, we need to navigate to **Manage | VM Storage Policies** while the VM is highlighted.

 In vSphere 6.0, the path will be **Monitor | VM Storage Policies**.

5. Once on the **VM Storage Policies** tab, you will be presented with a summary of the objects associated with the VM. These will include, at the very least, a **VM home** object (also called a *namespace* object or *Configuration file* depending on the context). In most cases, you will be presented with a **VM home** object and one or more VM disks:

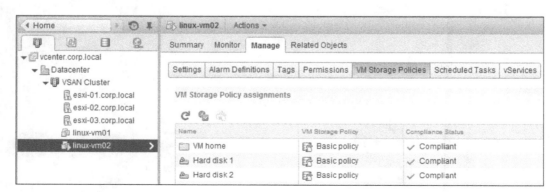

6. This will reflect which policy is applied to which object and whether this policy is compliant. This should match what you saw previously on the **Summary** tab.

7. To view the distribution of any given object throughout the VSAN cluster, select it from the list, and then view below the line to see the distribution:

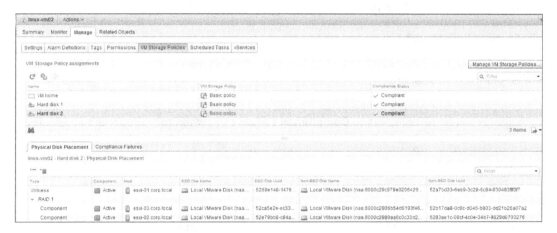

8. From here, you can see how the VM object is distributed and how fault tolerance is being maintained. For this example, we see that the VM has a simple RAID-1 layout with a single mirror and no additional striping per policy. There are two data components resident on **esxi-03.corp.local** and **esxi-02.corp.local**. There is a quorum-maintenance "witness" component on the **esx-01.corp.local** host. The panel will also display which specific disks are in use for these data objects and witnesses. In this way, we can see where the data actually resides and how VSAN has distributed objects to ensure that we can tolerate the loss of any given host in the VSAN cluster and still maintain availability.

How it works...

VSAN autonomously maintains storage policy selections during normal operation. To enable you as the administrator or architect of the system to examine what VSAN is doing, the SPBM agents on vCenter Server periodically poll the VSAN VASA provider on the VSAN master node. SPBM then takes this information and populates it in its database and makes it available to vSphere Web Client. When you select the VM from your inventory tree, this data is fetched and displayed.

There's more...

Because this data is populated on the basis of a poll, what you see in vSphere Web Client could be out of date. If you notice that the **Last Checked Date** field on the **Summary** tab is old, or if you have recently experienced some sort of VSAN outage event, such as the loss of a host, you can manually refresh the data by clicking on the blue circular **Refresh** button on the **VM Storage Policies** tab.

Due to visual layout constraints, this view may not reflect all the distribution details when a VM is running on a snapshot.

If a component is non-compliant against its specified storage policy, the reason for this non-compliance will be revealed in the **Compliance Failures** tab when the component is selected.

See also

▸   For more information about quorum maintenance and witnesses, please see the *Per-object quorum in VSAN* section of *Appendix B, Additional VSAN Information*

▸   For more details on the examination of compliance failures, please see the next recipe

▸   For more information about storage policies as they relate to VM snapshots, please see the *vCenter object distribution view and VM snapshots* section of *Appendix B, Additional VSAN Information*

Changing storage policies on a VM already residing in VSAN

Once a VM is created, you may find that you wish to alter the storage policy of the VM or one of its disks. This will typically be the result of the performance or availability requirements of a VM changing over time. For example, you may have a database or and e-mail server where you want the high-access data disks to be striped across physical spindles to help improve performance.

If changes need to be made, changes can be granularly applied to individual objects comprising the VM or to all components for the VM.

Getting ready

You should be logged into vSphere Web Client as an administrator or a user authorized to modify VMs.

How to do it...

1. In vSphere Web Client, navigate to **Home | Hosts and Clusters | Datacenter | Cluster**.

2. Select the VM that you wish to examine. For this example, we will examine the **linux-vm02** VM that we migrated to VSAN in the previous recipe.

3. Once the VM is selected, navigate to **Manage | VM Storage Policies**.

4. Click the **Manage VM Storage Policies** button:

5. If you wish to modify the VM storage policy for the entire VM, choose the applicable policy from the **Home VM storage policy** drop-down menu, and then click **Apply to disks**:

6. To change the policy on a specific disk, select the policy from the drop-menu next to the applicable disk, and then click **OK** to apply the change:

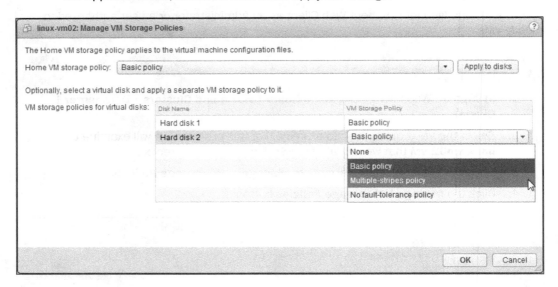

 Please note that the drop-down menu is hidden until you roll your mouse over the current storage policy, revealing the presence of the menu.

7. Once the new policy is applied, the **Compliance Status** column for the applicable objects will change to **Not Compliant**:

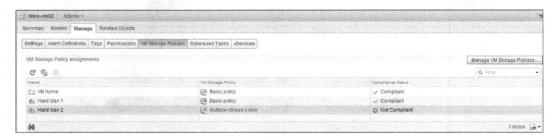

 Depending on the performance of your vCenter infrastructure, you may need to manually refresh the view with the circular blue refresh button on the **VM Storage Policies** tab.

8. With the non-compliant disk highlighted, you will see that the lower panel now reveals the changes being made to the VM disk, if applicable. In this example, we increased the stripe width from one stripe to two stripes. The **Physical Disk Placement** tab will thus reveal the following configuration:

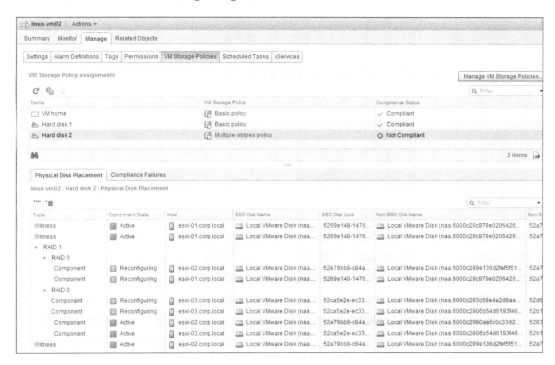

For now, the original single-stripe mirror still exists as the **Active** components, as does its witness. In addition, we now have a new set of RAID-0 devices that are being built across various disks and hosts. When this process finishes, the original RAID-1 mirror will be destroyed and production will continue seamlessly on the new RAID-10 mirrored stripes as defined in our storage policy.

Now, we will move on to the next method. This method applies only if you wish to change the storage policy of a VM disk. To change the storage policy of the VM home folder, you must use the previous method.

1. In vSphere Web Client, navigate to **Home | Hosts and Clusters | Datacenter | Cluster**.

2. Select the VM that you wish to examine. For this example, we will examine the **linux-vm02** VM that we migrated to VSAN in the previous recipe.

3. Right-click the VM and choose **Edit Settings...**:

4. In the resulting **Edit Settings** window, expand the options for the hard disk that you wish to change by pressing the small arrow to the left of the corresponding hard disk icon. This will reveal a drop-down menu for **VM storage policy**. You can expand this menu to select the new policy:

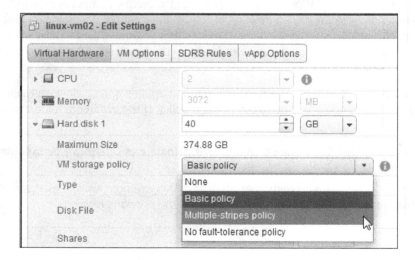

5. Once you have selected the applicable policy, click the **OK** button to apply your changes.

 You can also use this same step to apply different policies to various disks for VM creation or deploy-from-template operations. Identical options are presented to you in the **Customize hardware** step of a create/deploy operation.

 For monitoring object changes and to check compliance, please go to "Method 1" within this recipe and skip to Step 7.

How it works...

When you opt to modify the storage policy of the VM or the disks, your specifications are communicated to SPBM. SPBM then instructs VSAN to figure out how to modify the object(s) to bring them into compliance by communicating with the VSAN VASA provider on the VSAN master node.

There's more...

If VSAN determines that new components need to be created to satisfy the policy, it will determine how and where to place them. Once created, it will begin to migrate data from the existing components to the new ones. Status and component/object state changes will be communicated back to SPBM via the VSAN VASA provider. SPBM will then periodically poll the VSAN VASA provider, and any changes will be reflected in vSphere Web Client.

See also

▶ To learn how to get more details regarding the rebuild process, please see *Chapter 6, Ruby vSphere Console*

Modifying existing storage policies

Throughout the course of administering your vSphere/VSAN infrastructure, you may find that you wish to change a storage policy and the VMs associated with it. For example, you may want to change the amount of a VM that is thick-provisioned, or you may want to modify a policy so that it uses more stripes or provides a greater degree of fault tolerance.

By modifying an existing policy, you will cause these changes to cascade down to all VMs or VM disks that use the policy; thus, affecting many changes at once.

Getting ready

You should be logged into vSphere Web Client as an administrator or a user authorized to modify VM storage policies and VMs.

How to do it...

1. From vSphere Web Client, navigate to **Home | VM Storage Policies**.
2. Highlight the policy that you wish to modify, and then click the **Edit** button:

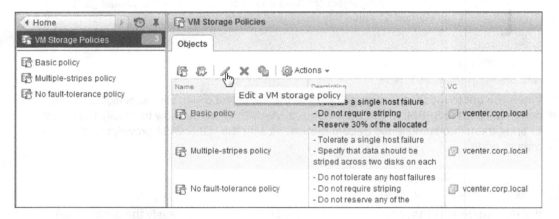

3. If you wish to modify the name or description, please do so, and then click **Rule-Set 1**.
4. Add the capability that you wish to use or modify one of the existing settings. In this example, we will increase the **Object space reservation (%)** value to 50%:

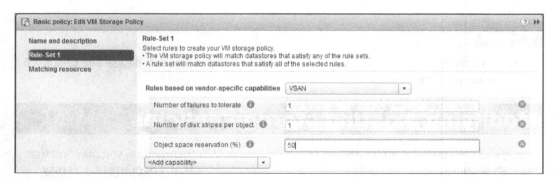

5. Click **OK** to update your storage policy. When you make this change, the wizard will inform you that your changes will affect the associated VMs. You will be prompted to apply the policy to VMs immediately or manually at a later time.

You may choose either option and then click **Yes**. For the purposes of this recipe, however, we choose to apply the policy manually to demonstrate the corresponding steps:

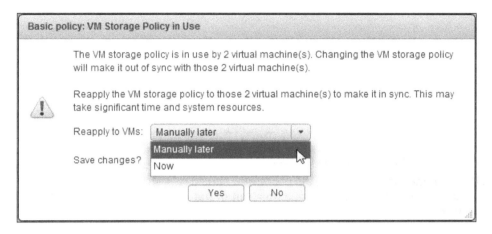

6. Navigate to **Home | Hosts and Clusters | Datacenter | Cluster | VM | Manage | VM Storage Policies**.

7. You will find that anything using the policy that we modified will reflect that the policy compliance status is **Out of Date**:

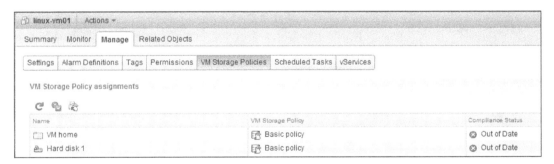

8. Click the **Reapply policy** button to apply the changes to the affected objects for the VM:

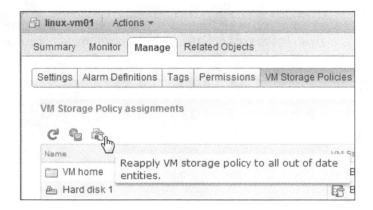

9. When prompted, click **Yes** to proceed with reapplying the storage policy.

10. When the task completes, the policy view should refresh. You will find that the compliance status has changed from **Out of Date** to either **Compliant** or **Not Compliant**, depending on whether or not the object needs to be reconstructed to satisfy the new criteria:

 Depending on the performance of your vCenter Server, you may need to click the circular blue refresh button.

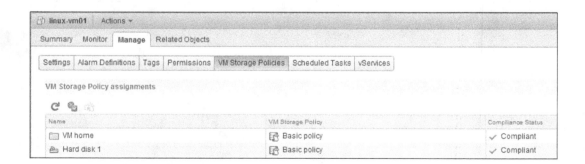

 If the compliance status changes to **Not Compliant** and you wish to learn more, please refer to the *Changing storage policies on a VM already residing in VSAN* recipe within this chapter. In particular, please see *Method 1, Step 7* and beyond.

How it works...

What happens in this case is extremely similar to what happens when we apply a new policy to a VM and/or a VM disk. The key differences are that, in this instance, we are reapplying an *already-associated* policy rather than applying a *new* policy, and we can make the change to many VMs simultaneously should we choose to do so.

There's more...

Depending on what changes are being made, the storage policy reapplication process can be very expensive in terms of time-to-completion and I/O load within the VSAN cluster. Changes that will require complete reconfiguration of the underlying objects include addition of mirrors (increasing the *failures to tolerate* value) and changes to the number of stripes. Changes to the object space reservation value may cause a full reconfiguration if VSAN's distribution logic that determines whether a full reconfiguration is necessary. If the policy change is likely to require that the associated objects be reconfigured and you have many VMs associated with this policy, it may be beneficial *not* to apply the changes in bulk. If you wish to modify the policy used by a specific VM or VM disk rather than all VMs associated with the policy, changing the policy for this particular VM is recommended as opposed to modifying the policy itself, which will affect all associated VMs.

While VSAN will scale back reconfiguration/rebuild I/O to help avoid crowding out production I/O, VSAN does insist that reconfigure/rebuild processes consistently make forward progress to prevent the possibility that a reconfigure/rebuild operation never completes. If the changes are significant and widespread, there is the possibility of production I/O slowing down to accommodate the large-scale change activity. This possibility can be obviated by staging in significant changes rather than applying them all at once. To apply the changes to VMs after modifying the policy, please use the **Manually Later** option after modifying the policy and refer to Steps 6–9 of this recipe.

Summary

Storage policies give you granular control over how the data for any given VM or VM disk is handled.

Storage policies allow you to define how many mirrors (RAID-1) and how many stripes (RAID-0) are associated with any given VM or VM disk.

Storage policies are applied at VM creation to begin with and can be changed later as the reliability or performance needs change.

The policies themselves can be modified if all associated VMs need to be changed in the same way.

If no policies are defined, VSAN will use its default policy to provide simple protection to any VMs created without explicitly defined policies.

4

Monitoring VSAN

In this chapter, we will discuss the following topics, with a recipe for each:

- ► Examining VSAN datastore health
- ► Examining VSAN disk health
- ► Examining VM object health
- ► Creating VSAN-specific alarms
- ► Examining VSAN resync activity (vSphere 6.0

Introduction

Once VSAN is deployed and in production, you will want to be able to monitor the health and capacity of the cluster, disks, and VMs and their various components.

This chapter will describe the GUI-based monitoring elements of Virtual SAN, and will show you how to monitor the high-level health of the cluster and create useful alarms to notify you of issues within your VSAN deployment.

In VSAN, many of the cluster monitoring features are available via the special command-line environment called the **Ruby vSphere Console** (**RVC**). While this chapter will cover monitoring options in the vSphere Client, please see *Chapter 6, Ruby vSphere Console* for a guide to more-robust monitoring tools in RVC.

Examining VSAN datastore health

Within VSAN, datastore health is the key to ensuring production continues without any problems. The most important aspect of overall datastore health involves free capacity

It is recommended that the VSAN datastore contain 20 percent free space to enable ideal placement decisions and effective rebalancing of storage objects.

Getting ready

▶ Your VSAN should be deployed and functional as per *Chapter 2, Initial Configuration and Validation of Your VSAN Cluster*.

▶ You should be logged in to the vSphere Web Client as an administrator or as a user with view datastore information

How to do it...

1. From the vSphere Web Client, navigate to **Home | Storage | VSAN Datastore**.
2. Click on the **Summary** tab.
3. Examine the capacity and number of connected hosts. You should find that the capacity is consistent with the aggregated size of your disk groups, and that the correct number of hosts is connected to the datastore.

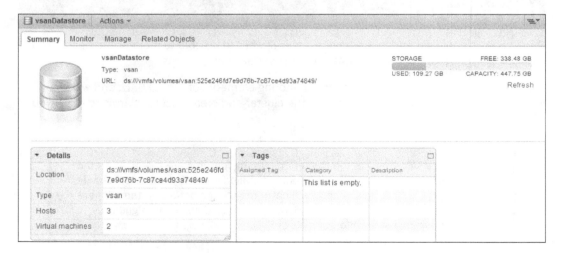

 If the capacity is inconsistent with the number of capacity-tier disks in the cluster, there may be a network partition in the cluster.

To examine datastore problems, we can examine alarms and triggered issues regarding the VSAN datastore. In the vSphere Web Client, click on **Home | Storage | VSAN Datastore | Monitor | Issues | All Issues**.

 In this example, there are no alarms or reported issues with the VSAN datastore.

How it works...

As VSAN is integrated into the vCenter Server, it uses the same monitoring and alarm paradigms as other aspects of vSphere.

There are other ways of getting more information about VSAN from the vSphere Client, but these views provide a high-level snapshot of the datastore health.

Examining VSAN disk health

As VSAN is a distributed storage solution, the health of disks and SSD devices in VSAN is essential to the operating health of the cluster. While we will go into the creation of VSAN-specific alarms (to help stay ahead of the curve) in a later recipe, we can examine the health of all disk groups and devices across the cluster via the vSphere Web Client.

Getting ready...

You should be logged in to the vSphere Web Client as an administrator or a user, permitted to view VSAN disk information.

How to do it...

Navigate to **Home | Hosts and Clusters | Datacenter | Cluster | Manage | Settings | Virtual SAN | Disk Management**.

Any disk groups that have a problem will have a red exclamation mark superimposed on the icon to indicate a problem. If there are any unhealthy disk groups, you can select them to determine which disk(s) have a problem.

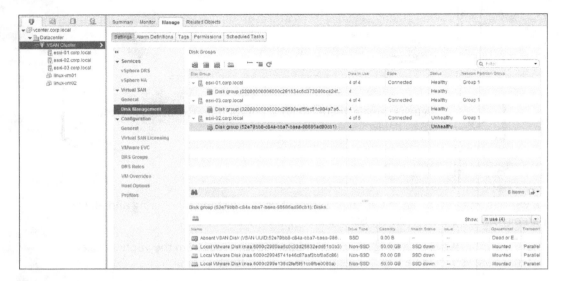

In this example, we see that the entire disk group on host 02 is unhealthy due to a failure involving the SSD.

How it works...

The health of the disk group is based on the health of the disks and SSD within that group. The overall health of the group is inherited from the health of the disks and SSD—any error on a disk or an SSD will result in an alarm on the disk group as a whole.

The relationship between the status of the disks or SSD will be reflected in the details. In the preceding example, the SSD has failed and thus the spinning disk health reflects **SSD Down**—the disk group is unavailable because the cache device died.

When introducing VSAN into an existing infrastructure, you may have existing VMs that reside on external storage such as NFS, iSCSI, or Fibre Channel.

Examining VM object health

Even if there are no alarms or disk failures in VSAN, you may wish to examine the specific VMs residing on VSAN storage. The VMs and their disks can periodically change distribution as VSAN load-balances. If there is a problem in a disk group, it will likely affect at least one VM as you increase the number of VMs, so examining the VM will give you a high-level view of any activity or issues associated with the VM.

Getting ready...

You should be logged in to the vSphere Web Client as an administrator or a user permitted to view VM configuration details.

How to do it...

1. In the vSphere Web Client, navigate to **Home** | **Hosts and Clusters** | **Datacenter** | **Cluster**.

2. Select the VM you wish to examine. For this example, we will examine the **linux-vm02** VM.

3. Navigate to **Manage** | **VM Storage Policies** while the VM is highlighted.

 In vSphere 6.0, the path will be **Monitor** | **Policies** | **Storage**

4. Once you are on the **VM Storage Policies** tab, you will be presented with a summary of the objects associated with the VM and their compliance statuses.

5. Any noncompliant objects will be marked. When it is selected, you will see if there are any problems with the object as well as any current activity.

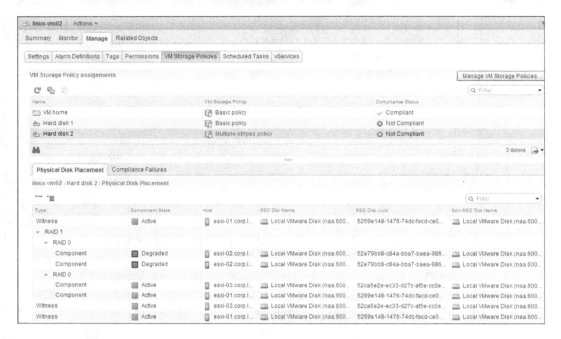

In this example, you can see that the object is available but noncompliant because there is a missing mirror. Two components for the object are in a **Degraded** state, meaning they reside on a dead disk. This is due to the failed SSD that was demonstrated in the previous recipe.

Once a failure has been remedied (or if there are enough capacity and hosts to allow a rebuild to begin, prior to repairing the problem), you will also see more specific information regarding object health and status:

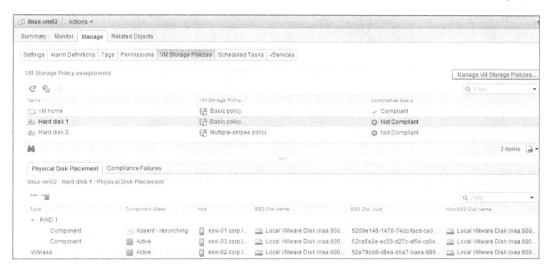

In this example, you can see that we have resolved the disk problem and the component, rather than being **Degraded** as in the previous example, is now in a **Resynching** status.

How it works...

vCenter Server works in tandem with VSAN to provide the status of objects associated with VMs via the vSphere Web Client. When you request information about the VM and its objects by selecting the VM or refreshing the **VM Storage Policies** view, vCenter and VSAN will provide the current state of the objects.

There's more...

In the vSphere Web Client, you are most likely to see the following states:

- ▶ **Active**: the component is normal and healthy.

- ▶ **Absent**: the disk or node on which the component resides is unavailable. This state is common during maintenance operations.

- ▶ **Absent - resynching**: the disk or node on which the component resides is now available and VSAN is performing a resynchronization to bring the object back into compliance.

- ▶ **Degraded**: The disk (or disk group) on which the component resides is dead.

- ▶ **Reconfiguring**: A dead component is being rebuilt elsewhere, or the object is being rebuilt to reflect a change in storage policy.

Creating VSAN-specific alarms

When using VSAN for production purposes, there are a few alarms that can be created in vCenter to notify you when specific conditions are encountered. This allows you to be more proactive with your monitoring of VSAN health. It is strongly encouraged that VSAN-specific alarms be created when running in a production environment.

 The recipe reflects the process used to add an alarm for VSAN. The specific alarm definitions will be found in the *There's More...* section and the source of this information will be found in the *See also* section.

Getting ready

You should be logged in to the vSphere Web Client as an administrator or user authorized to view and create alarms.

How to do it...

1. In the vSphere Web Client, navigate to **Home | Hosts and Clusters | vCenter | Manage | Alarm Definitions**.

2. Click on the green **+** icon to create a new alarm.

3. In the resulting wizard, make the following changes:

    ❑ **Alarm name**: <enter a descriptive, meaningful name for the alarm>

    ❑ **Description**: <enter a verbose description of what the alarm does, if desired>

    ❑ **Monitor**: Hosts

    ❑ **Monitor for**: a specific event occurring on this object—for example, VM power on

The **Enable this alarm** box should be checked.

4. Click on **Next**.

5. On the **Triggers** step in the wizard, click on the green **+** button to create a new trigger.

6. Enter or paste the event string into the box and strike *Enter*.

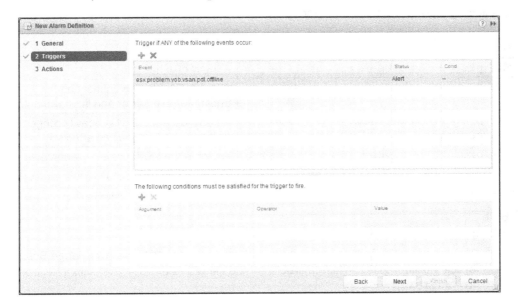

7. Click on **Next**.

8. On the **Actions** step in the wizard, click on the green **+** button to define the actions that vCenter should take if the alarm triggers. These include e-mailing the administrator, sending an SNMP trap, and so on.

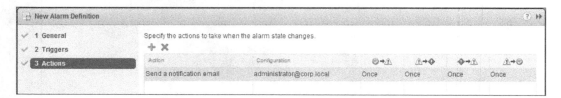

9. Click on **Finish** to create the alarm.

How it works...

With these steps, we are integrating additional conditional triggers into the existing vCenter alarm infrastructure. When these VSAN-specific events occur, a *VMkernel Observation Event* occurs. vCenter, through its agents on the host, detects these events and notifies vCenter. Once the alarm is created, vCenter subsequently triggers an alarm to notify you when the agents detect these specific Observation Events.

There's more...

The following alarms can be created for VSAN:

Event name	Description
`esx.problem.vob.vsan.pdl.offline`	A VSAN disk has gone offline
`esx.problem.vob.vsan.lsom.diskerror`	A VSAN disk, though online, has encountered an error and is unavailable
`esx.problem.vsan.lsom.congestionthreshold`	An SSD used in VSAN is heavily congested and performance may be affected
`esx.problem.vob.vsan.lsom.componentthreshold`	A host in the VSAN cluster is approaching the maximum number of components it can manage.

See also

▶ The event names for this recipe were gathered from the VMware Knowledge Base, article number 2091347. This article can be viewed at `http://kb.vmware.com/kb/2091347`.

Examining VSAN resync activity (vSphere 6.0)

Monitoring VSAN resync activity in vSphere 5.5 involves the use of the Ruby vSphere Console (RVC); in vSphere 6.0, the process can be monitored directly in the vSphere Web Client. This addition to the vSphere Web Client is available only with version 6.0.

Getting ready...

You should be logged in to the vSphere Web Client as an administrator or user entitled to view VSAN configurations.

How to do it...

From the vSphere Web Client, navigate to **Home | Hosts and Clusters | Datacenter | Cluster | Monitor | Virtual SAN | Resyncing Components**. Any resyncing components will be reflected in the window:

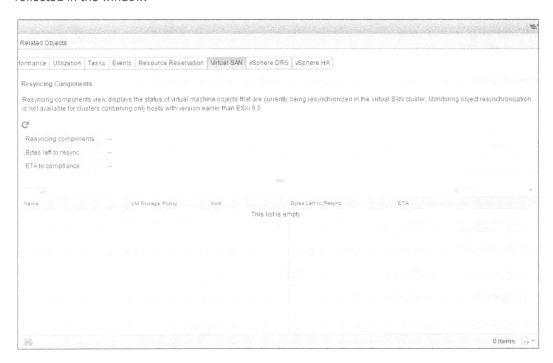

While there are no resyncing components in this example, you can see how much data is left to sync and how long the operations will take to complete. Any VMs associated with syncing components will be listed in the lower pane.

How it works...

Internally, VSAN keeps track of all component states at all times. Whether a component is missing, damaged, synchronizing, and so on, VSAN keeps a record of what is going on within the cluster. In this way, VSAN is able to respond to adverse events and proactively relocate/ rebalance objects throughout the cluster. This new view in vSphere 6.0 enables the vSphere Web Client to display a piece of this data that is continuously managed by the VSAN cluster.

There's more...

While this view has been added to vSphere 6.0, you can still monitor for resyncing components using the **Ruby vSphere Console** (**RVC**). RVC is outlined in *Chapter 6*, *Ruby vSphere Console*.

5

VSAN Maintenance Operations

In this chapter, we will discuss the following topics, with a recipe for each:

- ▶ Understanding and using VSAN Maintenance Mode
- ▶ Adding disks to VSAN
- ▶ Removing disks/disk groups from VSAN
- ▶ Replacing disks in VSAN in the event of a disk failure
- ▶ Changing VSAN networking
- ▶ Permanently decommissioning a VSAN node
- ▶ Recovering a VSAN cluster in the event that vCenter is lost/migrating a VSAN cluster to a new vCenter Server

Introduction

As with any production system, VSAN will require periodic maintenance. Drivers and system firmware will need to be updated, new releases of vSphere will ship, and various configuration changes or hardware updates will need to be performed. You may want to expand or contract the amount of storage available to VSAN, add or subtract nodes, or make various other modifications to your infrastructure.

As VSAN is a converged infrastructure solution that merges the compute and storage aspects of your IT environment, there are special considerations for VSAN maintenance. When performed properly, VSAN maintenance operations will proceed in a seamless way and be free of any outage-causing or other generally deleterious events.

There are numerous VSAN-specific maintenance tasks.

Addition of new nodes is not covered here via a recipe, since most of the information is redundant against *Chapter 2, Initial Configuration and Validation of Your VSAN Cluster*. To reduce the duplication of content, this procedure will be discussed in the *VSAN cluster expansion* section of *Appendix B, Additional VSAN Information*.

Understanding and using VSAN Maintenance Mode

As VSAN is fully integrated into your regular vSphere deployment and the VSAN maintenance mode is integrated into the regular vSphere ESXi maintenance mode. When VSAN is active on a host and a cluster, new maintenance mode options are presented to specify how you want to handle data availability when using a maintenance mode in your VSAN-enabled infrastructure. Making maintenance mode decisions consistent with the goal of your operation will help streamline the maintenance process and avoid inadvertent storage-related outages.

Special VSAN maintenance mode options are not available in the legacy vSphere Client. You must use vSphere Web Client.

For the purposes of this recipe, we will use the **Ensure Accessibility** option for the VSAN maintenance mode in the examples. For a complete description of all VSAN maintenance mode options, please see the *There's More...* section in this recipe.

Getting ready

You should be logged into vSphere Web Client as an administrator or a user authorized to change the host's VSAN maintenance mode state.

How to do it...

1. In vSphere Web Client, go to **Home | Hosts and Clusters | Datacenter | VSAN Cluster | Host**.

2. If you are not using vSphere DRS, or if DRS is not in an automatic mode, migrate all running VMs to other hosts in the cluster.

3. Right-click the host and choose **Enter Maintenance Mode**.

In vSphere 6.0, right-click the host and go to **Maintenance Mode | Enter Maintenance Mode**.

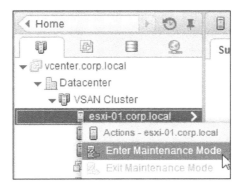

4. This will launch a new dialog box where you must specify your maintenance mode options. This box has the traditional option to migrate powered-off/suspended VMs, as well as the new VSAN-specific options.

   Select the applicable VSAN option from the drop-down menu, and then click **OK**.

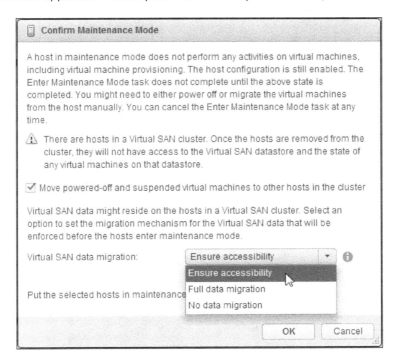

5. Acknowledge any subsequent dialog boxes involving migration and so on.

6. A maintenance mode operation will begin. In VSAN, maintenance mode operations can take quite some time depending on the maintenance mode type you specified. If data migration is needed, this must be completed before the operation finishes and maintenance can begin. The host will remain in the **Enter Maintenance Mode** state until the operation completes.

 You can monitor the progress of the maintenance mode operation in the **Recent Tasks** pane in vSphere Web Client.

There's more...

VSAN gives you three options for maintenance mode operations. These options are as follows:

▶ **Ensure Accessibility**: This is the default option for the VSAN maintenance mode. VSAN's internal logic will determine which (if any) components will need to be replicated/resynchronized to ensure that all VMs remain accessible during the host outage. Only accessibility is considered, and this option will result in the least data movement while guaranteeing VM accessibility and production.

▶ **Full data migration**: This option will evacuate all data from the node entering the maintenance mode, even if this migration is not required to maintain accessibility. This option is most useful if you are decommissioning a node or if you are anticipating an extended outage.

▶ **No data migration**: No data will be evacuated and the host will immediately enter the maintenance mode. This option is closest to the traditional vSphere ESXi maintenance mode. This option could cause an outage to the running VMs if they depend on this node for data service and the other nodes cannot service the data needs.

If VSAN is taking a long time to enter the maintenance mode, there may be data migration occurring. The maintenance mode operation can be cancelled if desired.

See also

Please see Chapter 4, *Monitoring VSAN*, and Chapter 6, *Ruby vSphere Console*, to learn how to monitor data resynchronization activities.

If you are anticipating an extended outage, you may wish to consider the **Full data migration** option. For more information, please see the *VSAN rebuild logic and maintenance* section in *Appendix B, Additional VSAN Information*

.

Adding disks to VSAN

As your infrastructure grows and your needs for capacity and/or performance changes, you may need to scale up your VSAN cluster by adding disks or disk groups to the existing VSAN nodes. This can be done online, and new disks/disk groups will be immediately available for provisioning, rebuild, and rebalance operations.

If you are in the auto-claim mode for VSAN disks (see *Chapter 2, Initial Configuration and Validation of Your VSAN Cluster*), VSAN will automatically claim any new disks and distribute them in the manner that it determines to be optimal. If you wish to override these decisions or manually define how your disks will be allocated, please disable the auto-claim mode. This process is outlined in the *Removing disks from VSAN* recipe in this chapter.

It is a strongly recommended best practice to maintain symmetry in the VSAN cluster. If you add disks or disk groups to one node, you should add the same number of disks of equivalent capacity to the other nodes in the cluster. New disk groups should ideally be of the same size as the existing disk groups.

Further, new disks being added to the existing disk groups should have the same capacity and type/performance profile as the disks already in the disk group.

Getting ready

You should be logged into vSphere Web Client as an administrator or a user authorized to alter VSAN configurations.

You should have already added your new disk(s) to the VSAN nodes and prepared them as RAID-0 devices and/or tagged them as SSD devices, if applicable.

How to do it...

1. Navigate to **Home | Hosts and Clusters | Datacenter | VSAN Cluster | Manage | Disk Management**.
2. Select the disk group that you wish to expand.

3. In the lower pane, click the green **+** button to bring up the wizard:

4. Any unclaimed disks not already in use for VSAN or as VMFS volumes or Raw Device Mappings will appear in a list. Check the box next to the disk(s) you wish to add, and then click on **OK**.

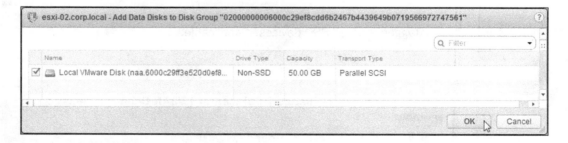

5. VSAN will claim and format the new disks then integrate them into the disk group for use. You can track the progress of this activity by monitoring the **Add local disks to Virtual SAN** task in the **Recent Tasks** panel.

Expand an existing disk group

1. Navigate to **Home** | **Hosts and Clusters** | **Datacenter** | **VSAN Cluster** | **Manage** | **Disk Management**.

2. Select the host to which you want to add a disk group.

3. Click the **Create a new disk group** button at the top of the upper panel.

4. In the resulting dialog box, select your SSD from the top pane and any spinning disks that you wish to use from the lower pane. Then, click on **OK**.

5. VSAN will claim and format the new disks and integrate the new disk group into your VSAN infrastructure. You can track the status of this activity by monitoring the **Create a new disk group** task in the **Recent Tasks** panel.

6. When the process finishes, you will see the new disk group listed under the host in the **Disk Management** view:

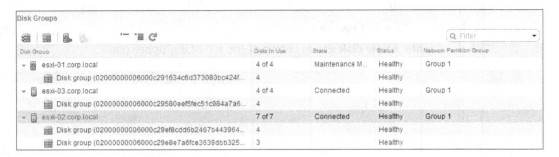

How it works...

This process is essentially the same as when we initially configured VSAN. The process that goes on beneath the surface is the same—the disks are formatted, claimed, and integrated into VSAN. Initially, these disks will be empty and unused by VSAN. This new capacity will initially be favored for new objects (newly provisioned VMs or VM disks) and VSAN will load balance the existing objects onto the new disks/disk groups over time.

See also

If you need to tag new disks as local devices and/or as SSDs, please see the *"Tagging disks as local solid-state drives (if applicable)"* recipe in *Chapter 2, Initial Configuration and Validation of Your VSAN Cluster.*

Removing disks/disk groups from VSAN

At some point during the course of your production and development with VSAN, you may wish to remove disks or disk groups from VSAN usage. For example, you may wish to upgrade your existing disks or otherwise repurpose them if VSAN is not capacity or performance constrained. While this process will probably be less common than adding capacity to VSAN, these operations can be executed via vSphere Web Client.

 If you are using vSphere 5.5, it is *strongly* recommended that you first place the host into maintenance mode by selecting the **Ensure accessibility** or **Full data migration** option.

Getting ready

You should be logged into vSphere Web Client as an administrator or a user authorized to alter VSAN configurations.

 To remove disks or disk groups, the VSAN cluster must not be in the auto-claim mode. If you need to change your auto-claim settings, please begin with *Disable auto-claim mode*. If you do not use the auto-claim mode, you may skip this section.

How to do it...

Disable auto-claim mode

 This step is only necessary if the VSAN cluster is using automatic disk claiming. If you are using manual disk claiming, you may skip this section.

1. In vSphere Web Client, navigate to **Home** | **Hosts and Clusters** | **Datacenter** | **Cluster** | **Manage** | **Settings** | **Virtual SAN** | **General**.

2. If you find that the **Add disks to storage** section reads **Automatic**, click on the **Edit...** button to change this behavior.

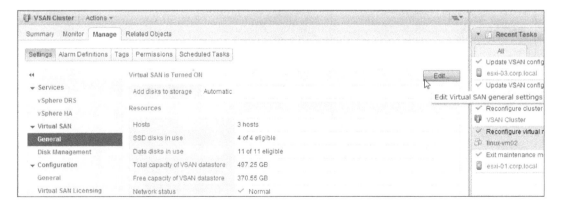

3. Select **Manual** from the **Add disks to storage** drop-down menu, and then click on **OK**.

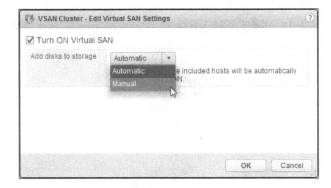

4. You can monitor the progress of this operation by using the **Recent Tasks** panel.

For removing a disk, follow these steps:

1. Navigate to **Home** | **Hosts and Clusters** | **Datacenter** | **Cluster** | **Manage** | **Settings** | **Virtual SAN** | **Disk Management**.

2. Select the disk group from which you wish to remove a disk.

3. From the lower panel, select the disk(s) that you wish to remove and click on the **Remove the selected disk(s) from the disk group** button:

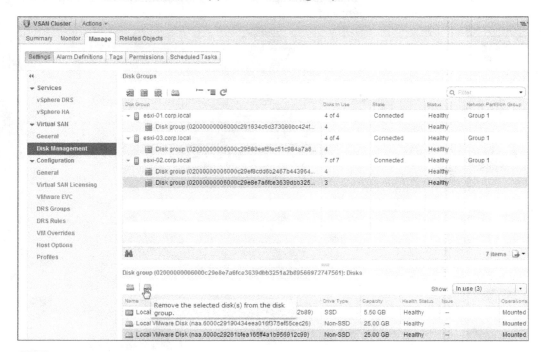

The subsequent behavior differs on the basis of the vSphere version.

- ❏ **vSphere 5.5**: The subsequent dialog box will notify you that the disk will be destroyed and this could subsequently lead to a loss of data if the data is not replicated or otherwise available on the other nodes. It is for this reason that we strongly recommend that you be in the maintenance mode prior to this operation. If you are sure that you wish to proceed, acknowledge this notification by clicking on **Yes**.

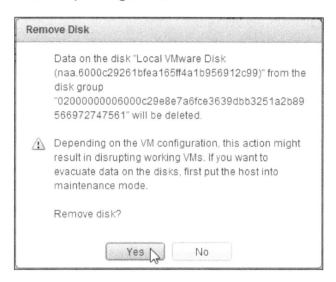

- ❏ **vSphere 6.0**: The subsequent dialog box will notify you that the disk will be destroyed. You will be presented with the option to migrate data prior to the removal of the disk, as well as how much data to move. *It is strongly recommended that you leave this box checked!* If you are sure that you wish to proceed, acknowledge this notification by clicking on **Yes**.

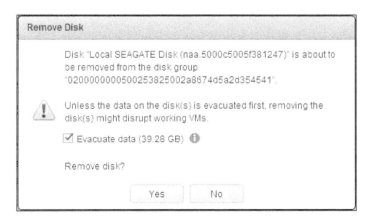

4. The disk will be removed. You can monitor the removal status by examining the **Recent Tasks** panel.

To remove a disk group, follow these steps:

1. Navigate to **Home | Hosts and Clusters | Datacenter | Cluster | Manage | Settings | Virtual SAN | Disk Management**.

2. Select the disk group that you wish to remove.

3. Click on the **Remove the disk group** button at the top of the upper panel:

The subsequent behavior differs on the basis of the vSphere version.

❏ **vSphere 5.5**: The subsequent dialog box will notify you that the disk group will be destroyed and this could subsequently lead to a loss of data if the data is not replicated or otherwise available on the other nodes. It is for this reason that we strongly recommend that you be in the maintenance mode prior to this operation. If you are sure that you wish to proceed, acknowledge this notification by clicking **Yes**.

- **vSphere 6.0**: The subsequent dialog box will notify you that the disk group will be destroyed. You will be presented with the option to migrate data prior to the removal of the disk group, as well as how much data to move. *It is strongly recommended that you leave this box checked!* If you are sure you wish to proceed, acknowledge this notification by clicking **Yes**.

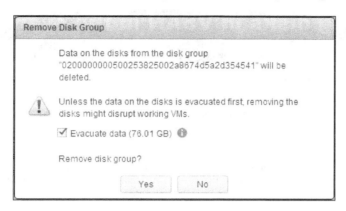

The disk will be removed. You can monitor the removal status by examining the **Recent Tasks** panel.

How it works...

If you choose to remove disks from use by VSAN, the data on these disks becomes unavailable. This process can result in a loss of production if any data depends exclusively on the disks/disk groups being removed. This is why there are a significant number of confirmation steps during this operation.

There's more...

In vSphere 5.5, disks are removed and the objects are subsequently rebuilt, akin to how VSAN would handle a disk failure. This is why one of the availability-guaranteeing maintenance mode options is strongly recommended prior to disk or disk group removal in vSphere 5.5.

In vSphere 6.0, this behavior is significantly improved in that the data from the disks or disk groups being removed will be migrated *prior* to the destruction of the disks or disk groups. This improved methodology means that the host does *not* need to be placed into the maintenance mode prior to the operation and that the objects are fully rebuilt prior to the removal, which does not leave your data exposed to a potential double fault during recovery.

See also

To monitor the rebuild progress for objects affected by the disk/disk group removal, please see *Chapter 4, Monitoring VSAN,* and *Chapter 6, Ruby vSphere Console.*

Replacing disks in VSAN in the event of a disk failure

Computer hardware inevitably fails, and this will eventually be the case for the disks in your VSAN infrastructure. When a disk fails in VSAN, the data resident on this disk will be rebuilt elsewhere in the cluster and the cluster capacity will be reduced. Failed disks should then be replaced to recover the available capacity and restore full fault tolerance in the VSAN cluster.

 If you are removing and replacing healthy disks because you are performing an upgrade, please follow the *Removing disks/disk groups from VSAN* and *Adding disks to VSAN* recipes in this chapter.

Getting ready

You should be logged into vSphere Web Client as an administrator or a user authorized to make VSAN configuration changes.

The faulty disk should have been physically removed from the server and replaced with a healthy device.

How to do it...

1. Navigate to **Home | Hosts and Clusters | Datacenter | Cluster | Manage | Settings | Virtual SAN | Disk Management**.

2. Locate the disk group with the failed disk and select it. The disk group with the failed disk should be marked with a red exclamation mark:

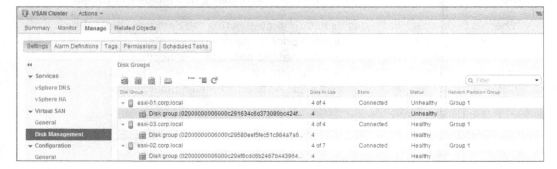

3. In the lower pane, select the **Absent** or **Failed** VSAN disk and click on the **Remove the selected disk(s) from disk from the disk group** button:

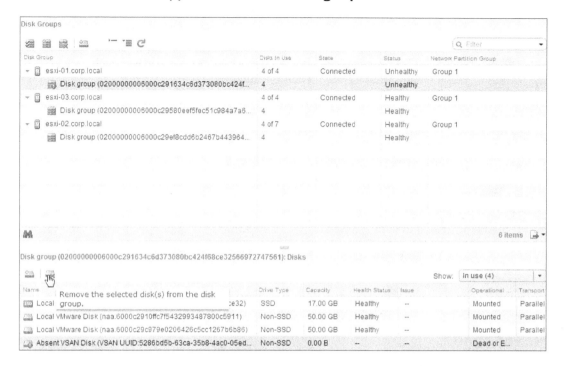

4. Confirm the operation in the subsequent dialog box. As the disk is already dead, no migrations can be attempted before removal.

5. To add the healthy replacement disk back into the cluster, please see the *Adding disks to VSAN* recipe in this chapter.

How it works...

This process is similar to the removal of non-failed disks that we discussed earlier in this chapter. The biggest difference here is that data migration via the maintenance mode and/or the vSphere 6.0 options are not applicable because the disk is dead.

Changing VSAN networking

Depending on how your environment evolves, you may find that you need to modify how VSAN operates on the network. By virtue of VSAN's distributed nature, networking changes require careful planning to avoid the potential of causing a network partition and/or a VSAN production outage.

If you are making any significant change, such as modifying the IP subnet or VLAN, the new networking should be configured alongside the legacy networking, and then the legacy networking can be removed once the new configuration is enabled.

> Even when taking all reasonable steps to avoid issues, networking changes could cause an outage if something goes wrong. Therefore, it is strongly recommended that significant network changes take place during a maintenance window.

In this recipe, we will demonstrate moving VSAN production to a new IP subnet. The same principle of standing up new networking before tearing down the original configuration applies to other similarly high-impact networking changes.

Getting ready

You should be logged into vSphere Web Client as an administrator or a user authorized to alter networking and VSAN configurations.

How to do it...

1. In vSphere Web Client, navigate to **Home | Hosts and Clusters | Datacenter | Host | Manage | Networking | VMkernel Adapters**.

2. Create your new VSAN vmkernel network interfaces. For the step-by-step procedure for this operation, please see *Chapter 2, Initial Configuration and Validation of Your VSAN Cluster*.

3. Complete steps 1–2 on all hosts in the VSAN cluster.

4. When you have completed, you will have two VMkernel interfaces created—the original VSAN interfaces and the new interfaces. In this example, we see the original interface in the IP subnet 10.100.100.0/24 and the new interface in the IP subnet 10.100.0.0/24:

5. Navigate to **Home | Hosts and Clusters | Datacenter | VSAN Cluster | Manage | Virtual SAN | Disk Management**.

6. Ensure that all hosts are still in the same **Network Partition Group**:

7. Navigate back to **Home | Hosts and Clusters | Datacenter | Host | Manage | Networking | VMkernel Adapters**.

8. Select your old/original VSAN network interface, and then click on the **Remove selected network adapter** button:

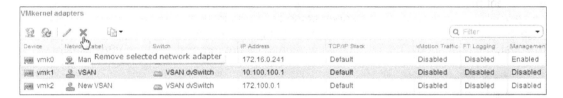

9. Confirm the operation in the subsequent dialog box:

10. Complete step 9 on all hosts.

11. Repeat steps 7 and 8 to confirm that all hosts are still in the same partition group following the change.

How it works...

The service binding between VSAN functions and VMkernel network interfaces can scale to multiple interfaces. While the preferred method to scale out the network is to use multiple physical uplinks in a port-channel or LACP link aggregate, we can bind multiple interfaces to VSAN. After binding the new interfaces alongside the original interfaces, VSAN will be able to use both of them simultaneously. Because the new interfaces are already in-place and in-use, we can safely remove the original interfaces. Any active traffic using the original interfaces will seamlessly fail over to the new interfaces.

In this way, we can make significant and fundamental changes to VSAN's network configuration without causing an outage, assuming that both network configurations work properly end-to-end.

Permanently decommissioning a VSAN node

You may find that you want to permanently remove a host from your VSAN cluster. The equipment might age out and get replaced or fail, or you may find that you don't need as much VSAN capacity and that the server could be more efficiently used elsewhere in the infrastructure. To avoid legacy information from lingering in the VSAN configuration and on the host, the host should be fully decommissioned before removal from the VSAN cluster.

Getting ready

You should be logged into vSphere Client as an administrator.

How to do it...

1. In vSphere Web Client, navigate to **Home | Hosts and Clusters | Datacenter | VSAN Cluster | Host**.

2. Place the host that you wish to decommission into the maintenance mode.

> As this is a permanent removal, please select the **Full data migration** option for the maintenance mode. If this is not possible due to inadequate capacity or very few nodes, choose the **Ensure accessibility** mode and immediately replace the node.

3. Destroy all disk groups on the host that you are decommissioning.

> See the *Removing disks/disk groups from VSAN* recipe in this chapter for more information.

4. Drag the host out of the VSAN cluster and put it in the root of the vCenter datacenter object. This removes the host from the vCenter cluster and the VSAN cluster:

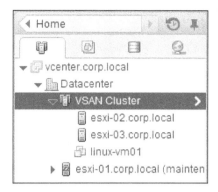

5. Destroy the VSAN VMkernel network interface on the host that you are decommissioning. Please see the *Changing VSAN networking* recipe in this chapter for more information.

6. Remove the host from vCenter or move it to its new cluster.

How it works...

When a host is part of a VSAN cluster, it knows about its own membership and all resources on this host associated with the membership (disks, network interfaces, etc.) maintain metadata about this relationship. To fully decommission a VSAN node, these resources and relationships need to be destroyed from the top down.

Starting with the maintenance mode, we move all data off a node and then destroy its disks. Once this is done, removing the host from the cluster cleans up the rest of the metadata related to the cluster node from the decommissioned node itself and the other nodes in the cluster. This ensures a clean removal.

Recovering a VSAN cluster in the event that vCenter is lost/migrating a VSAN cluster to a new vCenter server

If vCenter has failed and has been replaced, or if you need to move your VSAN cluster to a new/different vCenter Server instance, a new vCenter cluster should be prepared *prior* to the addition of the existing VSAN nodes to vCenter. If the procedure outlined in the recipe is not followed, it should not cause any production problems in VSAN, but it will result in warnings, failure messaging, etc., and certain operations may fail if VSAN licensing is not transferred.

Getting ready

This recipe assumes that the new vCenter server is built, licensed, and ready for use. A datacentre should already exist.

You should be logged into vSphere Web Client as an administrator.

How to do it...

1. From vSphere Web Client, navigate to **Home | Hosts and Clusters | Datacenter**.

2. Right-click the datacentre and select **New Cluster...**.

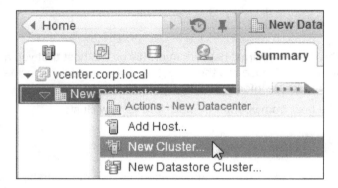

3. In the subsequent wizard, ensure that you enable Virtual SAN. If the cluster originally used vSphere HA and/or vSphere DRS, also enable these features on the new cluster:

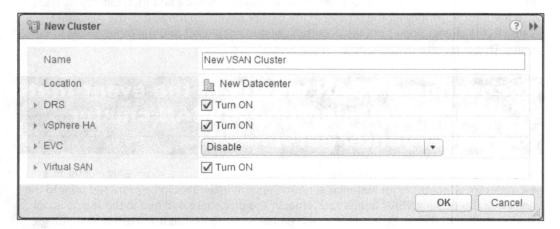

4. Ensure that the VSAN license is applied to the cluster. For more information, please see *Chapter 2, Initial Configuration and Validation of Your VSAN Cluster*.

5. Right-click the cluster and select **Add host....**

6. Proceed through the **Add host...** wizard. Ensure that you apply your host license when you add the host into the infrastructure.

7. Repeat step 6 for all hosts in the VSAN cluster.

8. Navigate to **Home | Hosts and Clusters | Datacenter | Cluster | Manage | Settings | Virtual SAN | Disk Management** and ensure that all hosts are present and normal:

 Important: Any storage policies that were in use prior to this operation will still be maintained and enforced by VSAN, but they will *not* be present in the new vCenter. To recover them, please see *Chapter 7, Troubleshooting VSAN*.

How it works...

vCenter will automatically discover and integrate VSAN information from the hosts when the hosts are added to the new vCenter instance. With the exception of previously defined storage policies, vCenter will pick up with VSAN seamlessly. It is for this reason that VSAN should be enabled on the cluster prior to adding the hosts to the new vCenter instance.

There's more...

If you were using vSphere Distributed Switches and vCenter was lost, the original dvSwitch will need to be restored from the backup if such a backup exists. If there is no backup of the dvSwitch, a new dvSwitch will have to be created, and the assets currently using the old dvSwitch will need to be migrated. Then, the old switch can be destroyed.

6
Ruby vSphere Console

In this chapter, we will discuss the following topics:

- ▶ Launching RVC (Windows vCenter)
- ▶ Launching RVC (Linux vCenter Appliance)
- ▶ Navigating RVC
- ▶ The vsan.cluster_info command
- ▶ The vsan.disks_stats command
- ▶ The vsan.vm_object_info command
- ▶ The vsan.vm_perf_stats command
- ▶ The vsan.resync_dashboard command

Starting with vSphere 5.5, VMware began shipping the **Ruby vSphere Console** (**RVC**) with the vCenter Server (Windows and Linux varieties). RVC is a command line utility, made for interacting with, managing, and monitoring various aspects of the vSphere infrastructure. Included with RVC are a large number of commands specific to VSAN monitoring and maintenance operations. The RVC interface will provide significantly more information about VSAN and its objects than can be determined from the vSphere Web Client alone. In addition, you can perform certain VSAN-related maintenance and troubleshooting tasks, which will be covered in the next chapter.

While RVC ships with the vCenter Server, it is also available for download from VMware Labs. For several reasons having to do with accessibility and resource consumption, it is strongly recommended to use RVC from somewhere other than the production vCenter Server. Some RVC functions, particularly VSAN Observer, can consume large quantities of memory, and so, externalizing RVC from the vCenter Server helps prevent possible resource contention. The easiest way to acquire an external RVC instance is to download the vCenter Server Appliance and deploy it for use as an RVC instance, as all requirements are already satisfied and the utility is already installed. As this appliance will not actually be used as a functioning vCenter, and will not be configured as such, there are no licensing considerations to this approach. The vCenter Server Appliance can be downloaded, deployed, and used just as an RVC instance.

If you wish to download RVC for manual installation or to download the vCenter Server Appliance, please see the various VMware web pages at `http://vmw.re/1JsmJxu` and `http://vmw.re/1kZqWXh`. While there is a lot more to RVC than simply VSAN commands, we will be covering some of the numerous VSAN-specific RVC commands and tools. We will not exhaustively discuss all VSAN operations or any non-VSAN RVC operations. We will go over the most useful operations and describe their outputs. More commands will be discussed in the troubleshooting chapter. All VSAN-related commands are named for what they do (provide information, query information, and so on) and begin with the string `vsan`.

> While we go over RVC invocation on both Windows and Linux, all example outputs will be created using a Linux RVC instance. All commands, syntaxes, and so on, are identical between the two flavors of RVC.

Launching RVC (Windows vCenter)

RVC for Windows as it ships with vCenter Server assumes you will be logging on as the local administrator. As this is rarely the case, we will modify the RVC invocation script prior to going through the launch/login process.

> This recipe assumes that the vCenter Server was installed to `C:\`. If you installed it in a different drive, please substitute the drive letters where appropriate.

Getting ready

You should be logged in to the vCenter Server via RDP or some kind of console.

Your user must be able to run applications as the Administrator on the Windows machine running RVC.

How to do it...

1. Navigate to `C:\Program Files\VMware\Infrastructure\VirtualCenter Server\support\rvc\` in Windows Explorer.

2. Make a backup copy of the `rvc.bat` file, as we will be modifying the original, as shown in the following screenshot:

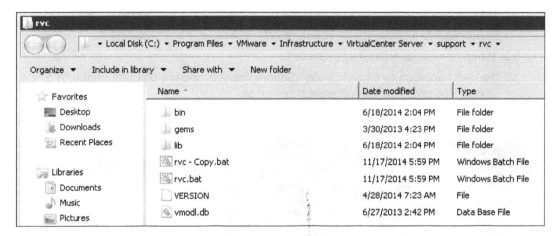

3. Launch a Notepad as administrator.

4. Open the `C:\Program Files\VMware\Infrastructure\VirtualCenter Server\support\rvc\rvc.bat` file for editing.

5. Initially, the the line in the batch file will end with `rvc Administrator@localhost`. Remove the `Administrator@localhost` part of the string and save the file.

 Ensure that you remove the space between `rvc` and `Administrator@localhost`.

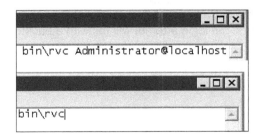

6. Save your work and quit Notepad.

7. Launch a command prompt as the administrator.

8. Navigate to `C:\Program Files\VMware\Infrastructure\VirtualCenter Server\support\rvc\`.

9. Type `rvc` and strike enter.

10. If prompted to accept a thumbprint, strike *y* to continue.

11. When prompted, enter your logon string in the form of `<username>@<domain>@<vCenter IP address or FQDN>`.

12. When prompted, enter your password.

13. You will successfully log in to Ruby vSphere Console and will be presented with a prompt, as shown in the following screenshot:

How it works...

The RVC modules are loaded through Ruby, and you then log into vCenter with your regular credentials. This connection is SSL-secured just like other vCenter communications.

There's more...

There was a behavior in the builds of RVC that ships with vCenter 5.5 and 5.5/U1, as well as the version that can be installed with `gem` where it is unable to parse a domain in your login string. If this problem occurs, the login attempt will fail with a backtrace, as shown in the following screenshot:

```
C:\Windows\system32\cmd.exe

C:\>rvc
Host to connect to (user@host): administrator@vsphere.local@172.16.0.240
C:/Ruby193/lib/ruby/gems/1.9.1/gems/rvc-1.8.0/lib/rvc/util.rb:62:in `err': inval
id URI (RVC::Util::UserError)
        from C:/Ruby193/lib/ruby/gems/1.9.1/gems/rvc-1.8.0/lib/rvc/uri_parser.rb
:47:in `parse'
        from C:/Ruby193/lib/ruby/gems/1.9.1/gems/rvc-1.8.0/bin/rvc:73:in `block
in <top (required)>'
        from C:/Ruby193/lib/ruby/gems/1.9.1/gems/rvc-1.8.0/bin/rvc:71:in `each'
        from C:/Ruby193/lib/ruby/gems/1.9.1/gems/rvc-1.8.0/bin/rvc:71:in `<top (
required)>'
        from C:/Ruby193/bin/rvc:23:in `load'
        from C:/Ruby193/bin/rvc:23:in `<main>'

C:\>
```

If this occurs, use a build of RVC that ships with vCenter 5.5/U2 or above, or set your domain as the default identity source in **Single Sign On** (**SSO**) and log in in the form of `<username>@<vCenter IP or FQDN>`.

RVC is backwards-compatible. RVC versions that ship with a vCenter major version or update release that is higher than the production vCenter version will be able to successfully connect to vCenter and will function normally.

See also

Changing the default identity source for SSO is outside the scope of this document. For that procedure, please see the official VMware documentation at `http://vmw.re/1GUzehA`.

Launching RVC (Linux vCenter Appliance)

Launching RVC in the vCenter Appliance is a one-stop operation. The modules are already compiled and available when you log into the appliance and can be launched from the default path.

Getting ready

You should be logged in to the vCenter Server Appliance via SSH or VM console as the root. It is strongly recommended that you use an SSH client such as the freely available PuTTY application to log in to the vCenter Appliance.

How to do it...

1. At the root prompt, type the following command and strike *Enter*:

   ```
   # rvc
   ```

2. When prompted for your username and password, enter it in the form of
   `<username>@<domain>@<vCenter IP address or FQDN>`.

3. If prompted to accept a thumbprint, please strike the *y* key.

4. When prompted, enter your password.

5. You will now be logged into RVC and presented with a command prompt, as shown in
   the following screenshot:

```
172.16.0.240 - PuTTY
vcenter:~ # rvc
Host to connect to (user@host): administrator@vsphere.local@vcenter.corp.local
password:
0 /
1 vcenter.corp.local/
> 
```

How it works...

The RVC modules are loaded through Ruby and then you log in to vCenter with your regular
credentials. This connection is secured, just like with use of the vSphere Client, PowerCLI,
or the vSphere Management Appliance.

There's more...

There was a behavior in the builds of RVC that ships with vCenter 5.5 and 5.5/U1, as well as
the version that can be installed with gem where it is unable to parse a domain in your login
string. If this problem occurs, the login attempt will fail with a backtrace:

```
C:\Windows\system32\cmd.exe
C:\>rvc
Host to connect to (user@host): administrator@vsphere.local@172.16.0.240
C:/Ruby193/lib/ruby/gems/1.9.1/gems/rvc-1.8.0/lib/rvc/util.rb:62:in `err': inval
id URI (RVC::Util::UserError)
        from C:/Ruby193/lib/ruby/gems/1.9.1/gems/rvc-1.8.0/lib/rvc/uri_parser.rb
:47:in `parse'
        from C:/Ruby193/lib/ruby/gems/1.9.1/gems/rvc-1.8.0/bin/rvc:73:in `block
in <top (required)>'
        from C:/Ruby193/lib/ruby/gems/1.9.1/gems/rvc-1.8.0/bin/rvc:71:in `each'
        from C:/Ruby193/lib/ruby/gems/1.9.1/gems/rvc-1.8.0/bin/rvc:71:in `<top (
required)>'
        from C:/Ruby193/bin/rvc:23:in `load'
        from C:/Ruby193/bin/rvc:23:in `<main>'

C:\>
```

If this occurs, use a build of RVC that ships with vCenter 5.5/U2 or above, or set your domain as the default identity source in **Single Sign On** (**SSO**), and then log in in the form of `<username>@<vCenter IP or FQDN>`.

RVC is backwards-compatible. RVC versions that ship with a vCenter major version or update release that is higher than the production vCenter version will be able to successfully connect to vCenter and will function normally.

See also

Changing the default identity source for SSO is outside the scope of this document. For that procedure, please see the official VMware documentation at `http://vmw.re/1GUzehA`. To download PuTTY, please see the PuTTY download page at `http://bit.ly/1jsQjnt`.

Navigating RVC

Once launched, RVC provides a shell-like method of navigating the vCenter inventory. It lays out vCenter objects in a filesystem-like hierarchy. This hierarchy follows the typical vCenter organizational model used by vCenter, which is visible through other tools like the Managed Object Browser.

For a more complete map of the vCenter inventory layout as it relates to RVC, please see Chapter 6 – *vCenter inventory layout* in RVC section of *Appendix A, Chapter-specific Expansions*. For the purposes of VSAN-related operations, we will primarily use the paths `root/<vCenter>/<Datacenter>/computers/<Cluster>` and `root/<vCenter>/<Datacenter>/computers/<Cluster>/resourcePool/vms`.

Navigation in RVC is accomplished with familiar *NIX commands for filesystem navigation. The `cd` command changes directories for navigation through the tree. The `ls` command lists the items available to you in the current location. `..` is the relative path to the parent directory. All commands require an inventory object against which it should execute. This is provided to the command as a path to the desired vCenter inventory object.

> RVC supports tab-completion, so typing paths or finding available objects in the next level is as easy as striking the *Tab* key.
>
> Like a *NIX shell, special characters such as spaces, must be escaped with a backslash (\) or quoted. Escapes are automatically inserted if you use tab completion.

Getting ready

You should be logged in to RVC as a vCenter administrator.

How to do it...

1. Once logged in to RVC, you are presented with a shell in the root of the inventory tree. The first inventory object is vCenter itself. You can change into it with `cd <vCenter Server>`. Then, you can see the available inventory objects by typing `ls`:

```
vcenter:~ # rvc
Host to connect to (user@host): administrator@vsphere.local@
vcenter.corp.local
password:
0 /
1 vcenter.corp.local/
> cd vcenter.corp.local/
/vcenter.corp.local> ls
0 Datacenter (datacenter)
/vcenter.corp.local>
```

> You'll note that the leftmost column contains a number. You can also use this number to move into the next level (for example, `cd 0` instead of `cd Datacenter`, in the example above). This navigation option can only follow an `ls` command. If you are navigating directly to an endpoint further along in the tree, you must use its actual name.

2. Here, we see that top level is the vCenter server, and the first vCenter objects with which we can interact are the datacenter(s) in your inventory. Like before, use `cd` to move into the datacenter object, and then `ls` to list the objects it contains:

```
/vcenter.corp.local> cd Datacenter/
/vcenter.corp.local/Datacenter> ls
0 storage/
1 computers [host]/
2 networks [network]/
3 datastores [datastore]/
4 vms [vm]/
```

3. Here, the inventory lists the various aspects of a datacenter—compute, network, storage, and VM assets. As clusters are primarily compute resources, you will find them enumerated under the `computers` level of the datacenter:

```
/vcenter.corp.local/Datacenter> cd computers/
/vcenter.corp.local/Datacenter/computers> ls
0 VSAN Cluster (cluster): cpu 7 GHz, memory 17 GB
/vcenter.corp.local/Datacenter/computers>
```

4. Here, we see the cluster called VSAN Cluster containing 7GHz and 17GB of compute and memory capacity.

5. Within the cluster, we see host resources in hosts and VMs are enumerated by resourcePool:

```
/vcenter.corp.local/Datacenter/computers> cd VSAN\ Cluster/
/vcenter.corp.local/Datacenter/computers/VSAN Cluster> ls
0 hosts/
1 resourcePool [Resources]: cpu 7.56/7.56/normal, mem
17.55/17.55/normal
```

6. From here, we can continue descending the tree into hosts to find hosts in the cluster, VMs/datastores/networks within a host, VMs within a datastore, and so on.

7. We can also descend the tree through resourcePool to find vms in the pool, VMs within resource pools or sub-pools, and so on.

8. We can ascend back one level by typing cd ..:

```
/vcenter.corp.local/Datacenter/computers/VSAN Cluster/hosts>
cd ..
/vcenter.corp.local/Datacenter/computers/VSAN Cluster>
```

9. We can ascend multiple levels in *NIX fashion with cd ../.. for however many levels are desired:

```
/vcenter.corp.local/Datacenter/computers/VSAN Cluster/hosts>
cd ../../../
/vcenter.corp.local/Datacenter>
```

10. We can return to the root in *NIX fashion with cd /:

```
/vcenter.corp.local/Datacenter/computers/VSAN Cluster> cd /
>
```

How it works...

Navigating RVC is directly analogous to navigating a filesystem on an *NIX system. The only difference is that instead of directories and files, you are navigating through the vCenter inventory using the filesystem-like construct.

The vsan.cluster_info command

While most cluster-related information can be obtained from the vSphere Web Client, the `vsan.cluster_info` command lays out all data about the cluster and its members, disks, networking, and many more, in one convenient list.

Getting ready

You should be logged in to RVC as a vCenter administrator.

How to do it...

1. As we are asking for information about the VSAN cluster, the command will be executed against the cluster level in RVC.

2. Type `vsan.cluster_info /<vCenter>/<Datacenter>/computers/<Cluster>` and strike the *Enter* key:

   ```
   > vsan.cluster_info
   /vcenter.corp.local/Datacenter/computers/VSAN\
   ```

```
> vsan.cluster_info /vcenter.corp.local/Datacenter/computers/VSAN\ Cluster/
Host: esxi-01.corp.local
 VSAN enabled: yes
 Cluster info:
   Cluster role: backup
   Cluster UUID: 525e246f-d7e9-d76b-7c87-ce4d93a74849
   Node UUID: 549609a5-0eb5-47ff-3000-005056830d58
   Member UUIDs: ["54966f69-5028-c54a-a906-005056830d58", "549609a5-0eb5-47ff-3000-005056830d58"] (2)
 Storage info:
   Auto claim: no
   Disk Mappings:
     SSD: Local VMware Disk (naa.6000c291634c6d373080bc424f68ce32) - 17 GB
     MD: Local VMware Disk (naa.6000c2910ffc6a6b61ffd7ea43d9973e) - 44 GB
     MD: Local VMware Disk (naa.6000c2910ffc7f5432993487800c5911) - 50 GB
     MD: Local VMware Disk (naa.6000c29c979e0206426c5cc1267b6b86) - 50 GB
 NetworkInfo:
   Adapter: vmk2 (10.100.0.1)
```

> The output about only one host is shown here to save space and avoid redundancy..

> If you have already descended through the inventory tree, you can always specify an execution point as your current location by typing a dot (.) to signify the current directory in *NIX fashion.
>
> For example, `/vcenter.corp.local/Datacenter/computers/ VSAN Cluster> vsan.cluster_info`.

3. Here, we can see that there are three members in the cluster (there are three member UUIDs listed), and the node, `esxi-01.corp.local`, is in the cluster backup role. It has three spinning disks and one SSD. The host uses `vmk2` for VSAN communication with the IP address of `10.100.0.1`.

How it works...

This command queries information about the cluster from each host and renders a list containing that information. This information included here, which is not accessible via the vSphere Web Client, includes the node UUIDs and roles.

The vsan.disks_stats command

While you can see which disks are included in a disk group, or where a VM is staged from the vSphere Web Client, you can get detailed disk utilization and distribution information from the table rendered by this command.

Getting ready

You should be logged in to RVC as a vCenter Administrator.

How to do it...

1. As we are asking for information about the VSAN cluster, the command will be executed against the cluster level in RVC.

2. Type `vsan.disks_stats /<vCenter>/<Datacenter>/computers/<Cluster>` and strike the *Enter* key:

```
> vsan.disks_stats /vcenter.corp.local/Datacenter/computers/VSAN\ Cluster/
2015-04-05 20:39:56 +0000: Fetching VSAN disk info from esxi-01.corp.local (may take a moment) ...
2015-04-05 20:39:56 +0000: Fetching VSAN disk info from esxi-02.corp.local (may take a moment) ...
2015-04-05 20:40:00 +0000: Done fetching VSAN disk infos
```

DisplayName	Host	isSSD	Num Comp	Capacity Total	Used	Reserved	Status Health
naa.6000c291634c6d373080bc424f68ce32	esxi-01.corp.local	SSD	0	11.90 GB	0 %	0 %	OK
naa.6000c2910ffc7f5432993487800c5911	esxi-01.corp.local	MD	5	49.75 GB	4 %	2 %	OK
naa.6000c29c979e0206426c5cc1267b6b86	esxi-01.corp.local	MD	1	49.75 GB	8 %	6 %	OK
naa.6000c2910ffc6a6b61ffd7ea43d9973e	esxi-01.corp.local	MD	0	43.75 GB	2 %	0 %	OK

The output about only one host is shown here to save space and avoid redundancy.

3. Here, we can see information about our disks. We can see what type of disk it is (**isSSD**), that we have components on all disks (**Num Comp**), how much of the disk is used (**Used**), and its state (**Status Health**).

How it works...

This command queries each host for disk information and then renders the table. As a result, the data provided here is effectively real-time. This view is extremely useful as it will show you distribution across the disks, how much of a disk is being used, and if your cluster is possibly imbalanced.

The difference between the **Used** and **Reserved** columns will reflect the differences between actual capacity consumed and the capacity that is reserved through the use of object space reservation policy options.

 As the SSD does not contain data components and is exclusively used for caching and buffering, it will always show **0%** used. This is normal.

The vsan.vm_object_info command

While you can see a VM's object distribution throughout the VSAN cluster by examining the Manage VM Storage Policies view in the vSphere Web Client, you can get more information about a VM's distribution and usage by examining the RVC command.

Getting ready

You should be logged in to RVC as a vCenter Administrator.

How to do it...

1. As we are asking for information about a VM running on VSAN, the command will be executed against the VM level in RVC.

2. Type `vsan.vm_object_info /<vCenter>/<Datacenter>/ computers/<Cluster>/resourcePool/vms/<VM>` and strike the *Enter* key:

```
> vsan.vm_object_info /vcenter.corp.local/Datacenter/computers/VSAN\ Cluster/resourcePool/vms/linux-vm02/
VM linux-vm02:
  Namespace directory
    DOM Object: 6a2b0d55-0f95-3137-54f1-005056831715 (owner: esxi-01.corp.local, policy: hostFailuresToTolerate = 1, stripeWidth = 1, spbmProfileId = d2f4cba3-4d21-41aa-a943-2fca6fca5b8a, proportio
nalCapacity = [0, 100], spbmProfileGenerationNumber = 0)
      Witness: 6b2b0d55-c7fd-5594-da0f-005056831715 (state: ACTIVE (5), host: esxi-01.corp.local, md: naa.6000c2910ffc7f5432993487800c5911, ssd: naa.6000c291634c6d373080bc424f68ce32,
        usage: 0.0 GB)
      RAID 1
        Component: 6b2b0d55-1f2f-5494-2e6e-005056831715 (state: ACTIVE (5), host: esxi-03.corp.local, md: naa.6000c2905b13e407b0c00f313a26ee43, ssd: naa.6000c29580eef5fec51c984a7a662bbc,
          usage: 0.1 GB)
        Component: 6b2b0d55-07e6-5194-bce1-005056831715 (state: ACTIVE (5), host: esxi-02.corp.local, md: naa.6000c2900aa6c0c33d26632edd51b0b3, ssd: naa.6000c29ef8cdd6b2467b4439649b0719,
          usage: 0.1 GB)
```

The output about only the namespace object (VM Home Directory) is shown here to save space and avoid redundancy.

3. Here, we see how the object is distributed, its policies, storage-policy UUID, and so on.

How it works...

This command queries VSAN for detailed information about the VM object distribution and its usage and makeup. Unlike in the vSphere Web Client, here, we can see actual on-disk space consumption (**usage:**), the UUIDs associated with object and components, and a complete RAID tree.

There's more...

A key benefit to this view versus the vSphere Web Client involves VMs running on snapshots. In the vSphere Web Client, only the top-level (for example, running snapshot) distribution is revealed. With this command, all snapshots and base disks will be revealed, along with their distributions and usages.

The vsan.vm_perf_stats command

While you can examine VM performance information via the vSphere Web Client, you can also get a quick at-a-glance view of VM performance using this command.

Getting ready

You should be logged in to RVC as a vCenter Administrator.

How to do it...

1. As we are asking for information about a VM, the command will be executed against the VM level in RVC.

2. Type `vsan.vm_perf_stats /<vCenter>/<Datacenter>/computers/<Cluster>/resourcePool/vms/<VM>` and strike the *Enter* key:

```
> vsan.vm_perf_stats /vcenter.corp.local/Datacenter/computers/VSAN\ Cluster/resourcePool/vms/linux-vm02/
2015-04-05 21:05:16 +0000: Querying info about VMs ...
2015-04-05 21:05:16 +0000: Querying VSAN objects used by the VMs ...
2015-04-05 21:05:17 +0000: Fetching stats counters once ...
2015-04-05 21:05:18 +0000: Sleeping for 20 seconds ...
2015-04-05 21:05:38 +0000: Fetching stats counters again to compute averages ...
2015-04-05 21:05:39 +0000: Got all data, computing table
+------------+-----------+-------------+---------------+
| VM/Object  | IOPS      | Tput (KB/s) | Latency (ms)  |
+------------+-----------+-------------+---------------+
| linux-vm02 | 1.1r/0.3w | 820.2r/0.2w | 365.0r/47.7w  |
+------------+-----------+-------------+---------------+
```

3. Here, we see the outcome of a recent sample of VM performance data. Not all possible counters are shown here, only a high-level view of I/O per second, Throughput and Latency.

How it works...

This command queries information about the VM and finds the objects associated with it, and then collects performance counters. The operation then suspends for 20 seconds and the performance information is fetched again. This raw data is then averaged and displayed to you.

This command is not particularly useful for long-term performance data, but it is excellent for acquiring an at-a-glance view of VM performance at the time that the command is executed.

The vsan.resync_dashboard command

One of the most important things you will need to keep track of as an administrator is the movement of objects throughout the cluster and keeping an eye on recovery/resync activity following failures or maintenance-related outages. This command will show you sync activity due to rebalance tasks, new policy application, and recovery operations.

This information is plumbed into the vSphere Web Client in vSphere 6.0, but it is only available through RVC in vSphere 5.5. This command still works in vSphere 6.0 and can provide additional information about non-VM related objects, which are still not revealed in the vSphere Web Client.

Getting ready

You should be logged in to RVC as a vCenter Administrator.

How to do it...

1. As we are asking for information about the VSAN cluster, the command will be executed against the cluster level in RVC.

2. Type `vsan.resync_dashboard /<vCenter>/<Datacenter>/ computers/<Cluster>` and strike the *Enter* key:

```
> vsan.resync_dashboard /vcenter.corp.local/Datacenter/computers/VSAN\ Cluster/
2015-04-05 21:07:22 +0000: Querying all VMs on VSAN ...
2015-04-05 21:07:22 +0000: Querying all objects in the system from esxi-01.corp.local ...
2015-04-05 21:07:24 +0000: Got all the info, computing table ...
+-----------------------------------------------------------------+------------------+---------------+
| VM/Object                                                       | Syncing objects | Bytes to sync |
+-----------------------------------------------------------------+------------------+---------------+
| linux-vm02                                                     | 1               |               |
|    [vsanDatastore] 6a2b0d55-0f95-3137-54f1-005056831715/linux-vm02.vmdk |          | 0.24 GB      |
+-----------------------------------------------------------------+------------------+---------------+
| Total                                                          | 1               | 0.24 GB      |
+-----------------------------------------------------------------+------------------+---------------+
```

3. Here, we can see that we have one object resyncing. It is the VMDK associated with **linux-vm02**, and there is **0.24 GB** left to sync.

How it works...

This command queries all VSAN objects to determine which ones are resyncing. It then queries information about the resyncing objects to find the name and path of the asset that depends on that object, and the amount of data that remains to be copied.

There's more...

If you want to monitor this operation without continuously rerunning the command, you specify the `-r` flag and specify a time, in seconds, for the refresh rate. The command will then create the table, wait the specified time period, and run again. This operation runs forever until you interrupt it by pressing *Ctrl + C*.

For example:

```
> vsan.resync_dashboard
/vcenter.corp.local/Datacenter/computers/VSAN\ Cluster/ -r 300
```

This will refresh the output every five minutes (300 seconds).

7

Troubleshooting VSAN

In this chapter, we will discuss the following topics, with a recipe for each:

- ▶ Investigating network partitions (with vSphere Web Client)
- ▶ Investigating network partitions (without vSphere Web Client)
- ▶ Investigating Storage Provider registration problems
- ▶ Investigating other SPBM problems
- ▶ Investigating VM provisioning or power-on failures
- ▶ Investigating disk failures
- ▶ Investigating VSAN performance with VSAN Observer

Introduction

As with any IT infrastructure, you will occasionally encounter problems in your VSAN implementation. VSAN is designed to always enforce and maintain the integrity and consistency of production data, but this does not mean that outages or even data loss are impossible. In combination with the alarms discussed in *Chapter 4, Monitoring VSAN*, this chapter can be used to investigate common problems with VSAN configurations, settings, or components to enable you to return the cluster to service.

The procedures outlined in this chapter are general and seek to address common problems with VSAN configurations. In the event that the steps outlined in this chapter are inadequate or you encounter a different problem, you may need to contact VMware Support or your third-party support provider. To prepare you for the best support experience, please see *Chapter 8, Support Success*.

Investigating network partitions (with vSphere Web Client)

Once you have VSAN configured and enabled, you may find that the hosts are not communicating with each other properly. As VSAN is a distributed storage system, it depends on healthy, functional networking to work properly. If you have a cluster where not all nodes can communicate via both unicast and multicast IP, then one or more nodes will be in a different network partition from that of the other node(s). To work as expected, all VSAN nodes must be in the same network partition.

If the VSAN cluster is partitioned, you may notice one or more of the following behaviors:

▶ The capacity of the VSAN Datastore is smaller than expected

▶ You have experienced an HA failover event

▶ One or more hosts report **Host cannot communicate with all other nodes in the VSAN enabled cluster** in vSphere Web Client:

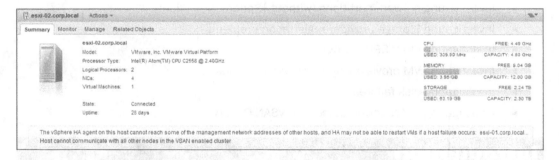

Getting ready

You should be logged into vSphere Web Client as an administrator.

How to do it...

1. First, verify that there is a network partition. In vSphere Web Client, navigate to **Home | Hosts and Clusters | Datacenter | Cluster | Virtual SAN | Disk Management**.

2. In the **Network Partition Group** column, determine whether more than one network partition is present:

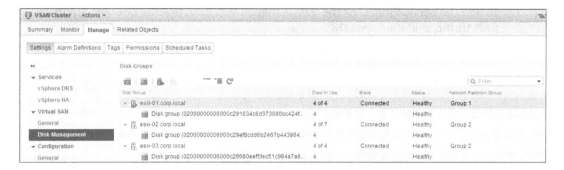

3. Once a network partition is confirmed, validate that all vmkernel network interfaces for use by VSAN are enabled for VSAN traffic. In vSphere Web Client, navigate to **Home | Hosts and Clusters | Datacenter | Cluster | Host | Manage | Networking | VMkernel adapters** and select the applicable interface.

4. We should find that the **Enabled Services** list includes Virtual SAN.

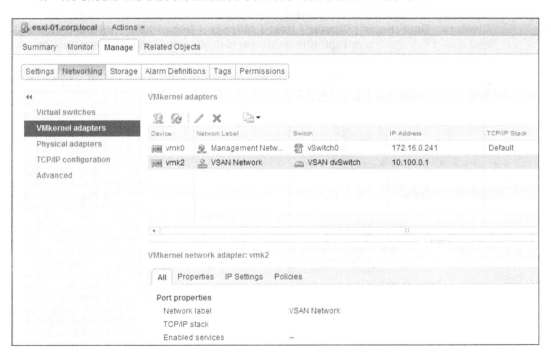

Here, we see that there are no enabled services; thus, the network interface is not tagged for use by VSAN.

1. To add the service tag, click the pencil-shaped edit icon, tick the box next to **Virtual SAN traffic**, and then click **OK**:

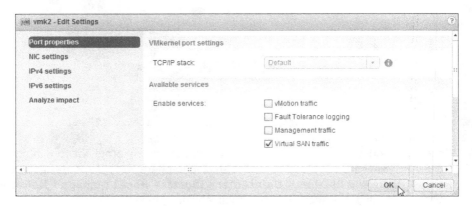

2. If all services are tagged properly, ensure that all VSAN vmkernel network interfaces are using the same VLAN. In vSphere Web Client, navigate to **Home** | **Hosts and Clusters** | **Datacenter** | **Cluster** | **Host** | **Manage** | **Networking** | **Virtual Switches** and select the vSwitch or Distributed vSwitch with which the VSAN-enabled vmkernel network interface is associated.

3. After locating the port group for the VSAN vmkernel interface, examine the **VLAN ID** field and ensure that the VLAN, if applicable, is correct:

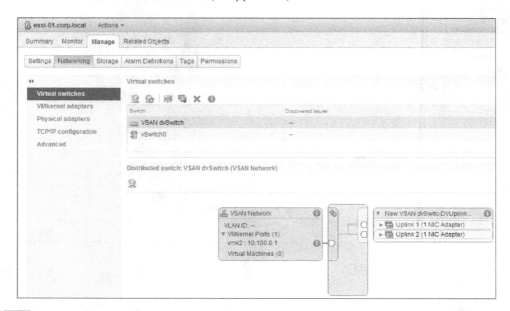

4. If the VLAN settings are correct, we should also validate the MTU for the vSwitch. In vSphere Web Client, navigate to **Home | Hosts and Clusters | Datacenter | Cluster | Host | Manage | Networking | Virtual switches**.

5. Select the applicable vSwitch and then click the blue-and-white information icon. In the subsequent dialog box, examine the MTU and make sure that it is as expected for your infrastructure:

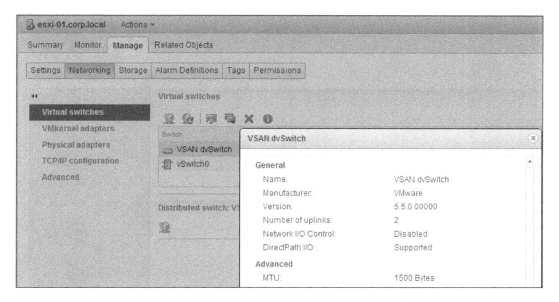

6. If the vSwitch MTU is correct, we should also validate that the vmkernel network interface is correct. If the vmkernel interface MTU is greater than the vSwitch MTU, it can cause communication problems including a VSAN network partition. In vSphere Web Client, navigate to **Home | Hosts and Clusters | Datacenter | Cluster | Host | Manage | Networking | VMkernel adapters**.

7. Select the applicable adapter and examine the settings to ensure that the interface MTU does not exceed the vSwitch MTU:

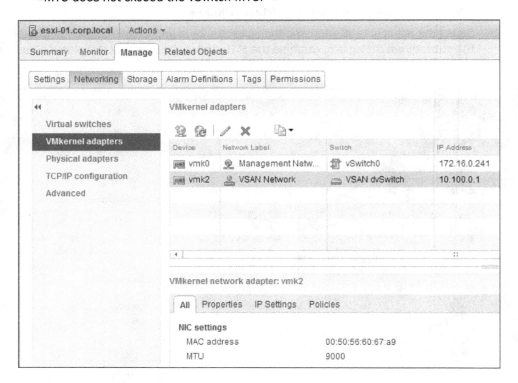

Here, we see that the MTU is 9000, which exceeds the MTU of the vSwitch.

If we are using an MTU of greater than the standard 1500 bytes, this also requires that upstream physical switches be configured to handle the larger MTU. It is a valid troubleshooting step to roll back the vmkernel interface MTUs to 1500 in order to determine whether it resolves the network partition. If it does, then the problem may be upstream.

8. If all vSphere-related networking settings (service tagging, MTU, VLAN, etc.) are valid and as expected, we should continue to investigate upstream. Ensure that the physical switch is configured to handle multicast IP traffic. This may require turning on IGMP snooping for the applicable VLAN and configuring IGMP queries or other settings.

How it works...

VSAN networking needs to be consistent across all VSAN nodes to ensure proper production. For this reason, the VLAN (if any), IP subnet, and MTU must all match across hosts and MTUs must be handled properly by all vSwitches and physical switches. To inform ESXi which interface to use for VSAN traffic, the applicable interface must be tagged for use by Virtual SAN.

Investigating network partitions (without vSphere Web Client)

Once you have VSAN configured and enabled, you may find that the hosts are not communicating with each other properly. As VSAN is a distributed storage system, it depends on healthy, functional networking to work properly. If you have a cluster where not all nodes can communicate via both unicast and multicast IP, then one or more nodes will be in a different network partition from that of the other node(s). To work as expected, all VSAN nodes must be in the same network partition.

If the VSAN cluster is partitioned and vCenter itself runs on VSAN-provisioned storage, you may not be able to investigate the problem by using vSphere Web Client. If this occurs, you should validate the network configurations via SSH or the physical console CLI. While choosing to run vCenter on VSAN-provisioned storage is a fully supported configuration and will not cause long-term production issues, it could make troubleshooting more complex in the event that vCenter itself is affected by the underlying issue.

Getting ready

You should be logged into the ESXi host(s) as the root via SSH or physical console.

How to do it...

1. First, verify that there a network partition. From the command line, run:

   ```
   # esxcli vsan cluster get
   ```

   If there is a network partition, we will find that fewer hosts than expected are listed in the Sub-Cluster Member UUIDs: section:

   ```
   ~ # esxcli vsan cluster get
   Cluster Information
      Enabled: true
      Current Local Time: 2015-04-10T09:24:31Z
      Local Node UUID: 54966f69-5028-c54a-a906-005056830d58
      Local Node State: MASTER
      Local Node Health State: HEALTHY
      Sub-Cluster Master UUID: 54966f69-5028-c54a-a906-005056830d58
      Sub-Cluster Backup UUID: 5496f643-fb36-5fda-d5c2-005056837d9f
      Sub-Cluster UUID: 525e246f-d7e9-d76b-7c87-ce4d93a74849
      Sub-Cluster Membership Entry Revision: 32
      Sub-Cluster Member UUIDs: 54966f69-5028-c54a-a906-005056830d58, 5496f643-fb36-5fda-d5c2-005056837d9f
      Sub-Cluster Membership UUID: 6c922755-0f9e-6b9e-a2ac-005056831715
   ~ #
   ```

   Here, we see that there are only two hosts listed under Sub-Cluster Member UUIDs when we are expecting there to be three entries, as this is a three-node cluster. Running this same command from the other hosts will identify the isolated node as it will have only one member. In the event that there are multiple nodes in each partition, we will be able to determine those relationships by finding which nodes can communicate with each other and isolate the cause of the communication failure (single node, top-of-rack switch, inter-switch communication, and so on.)

2. Once a network partition is confirmed, validate that all vmkernel network interfaces for use by VSAN are tagged for VSAN traffic. From the command line, run the following:

   ```
   # esxcli vsan network list
   ```

   If there is no output, then there is no interface configured for use by VSAN and the interface will need to be tagged.

3. To list the vmkernel network interfaces, run the following command:

   ```
   # esxcli network ip interface ipv4 get
   ```

   From the resulting output, locate the VSAN interface that you want to tag:

   ```
   ~ # esxcli network ip interface ipv4 get
   Name  IPv4 Address   IPv4 Netmask    IPv4 Broadcast  Address Type  DHCP DNS
   ----  ------------   ------------    --------------  ------------  --------
   vmk0  172.16.0.241   255.255.255.0   172.16.0.255    STATIC        false
   vmk2  10.100.0.1     255.255.255.0   10.100.0.255    STATIC        false
   ~ #
   ```

4. When you have identified the correct interface (vmk2 in this example), tag it for use with VSAN:

```
# esxcli vsan network ipv4 add -i vmk2
```

5. Once you have tagged the interface, re-run the network list command and observe the output:

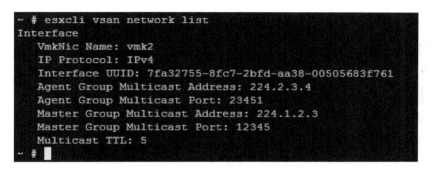

```
~ # esxcli vsan network list
Interface
   VmkNic Name: vmk2
   IP Protocol: IPv4
   Interface UUID: 7fa32755-8fc7-2bfd-aa38-00505683f761
   Agent Group Multicast Address: 224.2.3.4
   Agent Group Multicast Port: 23451
   Master Group Multicast Address: 224.1.2.3
   Master Group Multicast Port: 12345
   Multicast TTL: 5
~ #
```

6. If all services are tagged properly, ensure that all VSAN vmkernel network interfaces are using the same VLAN. To check the VLAN in use on a standard switch, run the following command:

```
# esxcli network vswitch standard portgroup list
```

Then, examine the output:

```
~ # esxcli network vswitch standard portgroup list
Name                    Virtual Switch   Active Clients   VLAN ID
--------------------    --------------   --------------   -------
Management Network      vSwitch0                      1         0
VM Network              vSwitch0                      1         0
~ #
```

7. If you need to modify the VLAN used by a standard port group, run the following command:

```
# esxcli network vswitch standard portgroup set -v
<portgroup_name> -v <VLAN>
```

Substitute the values for <portgroup_name> and <VLAN> as applicable to your infrastructure.

 VLANs for distributed switches cannot be modified from the CLI. If you need assistance with migrating VSAN networking to standard switches during outage-recovery efforts, please contact VMware Support or your third-party support provider.

8. If the VLAN settings are correct, we should also validate the MTU for the vSwitch. Run the following command:

    ```
    # esxcli network vswitch standard list
    ```

    or

    ```
    # esxcli network vswitch dvs vmware list
    ```

    Then, examine the output:

    ```
    ~ # esxcli network vswitch standard list
    vSwitch0
        Name: vSwitch0
        Class: etherswitch
        Num Ports: 1536
        Used Ports: 7
        Configured Ports: 128
        MTU: 1500
        CDP Status: listen
        Beacon Enabled: false
        Beacon Interval: 1
        Beacon Threshold: 3
        Beacon Required By:
        Uplinks: vmnic1, vmnic0
        Portgroups: VM Network, Management Network
    ~ # esxcli network vswitch dvs vmware list
    VSAN dvSwitch
        Name: VSAN dvSwitch
        VDS ID: d0 15 1d 50 58 bb 49 c9-b6 6f c5 79 a3 39 45 57
        Class: etherswitch
        Num Ports: 1536
        Used Ports: 6
        Configured Ports: 512
        MTU: 1500
        CDP Status: listen
        Beacon Timeout: -1
        Uplinks: vmnic3, vmnic2
        VMware Branded: true
        DVPort:
    ```

9. If the vSwitch MTU is correct, we should also validate that the vmkernel network interface is correct. If the vmkernel interface MTU is greater than the vSwitch MTU, it can cause communication problems including a VSAN network partition. Run the following command:

    ```
    # esxcli network ip interface list
    ```

Then examine the output for the MTU of the interface:

```
vmk2
    Name: vmk2
    MAC Address: 00:50:56:60:67:a9
    Enabled: true
    Portset: DvsPortset-1
    Portgroup: N/A
    Netstack Instance: defaultTcpipStack
    VDS Name: VSAN dvSwitch
    VDS UUID: d0 15 1d 50 58 bb 49 c9-b6 6f c5 79 a3 39 45 57
    VDS Port: 0
    VDS Connection: 864523842
    Opaque Network ID: N/A
    Opaque Network Type: N/A
    External ID: N/A
    MTU: 1500
    TSO MSS: 65535
    Port ID: 67108872
~ #
```

10. If you find that the MTU of the interface needs to be adjusted to match the vSwitch, run the following command:

    ```
    # esxcli network ip interface set -i <vmk_number> -m
    <MTU_size>
    ```

    Substitute the values for <vmk_number> and <MTU_size> as applicable to your infrastructure.

11. If you find that the MTU of the standard vSwitch needs to be adjusted to match the vmkernel network interface, run the following command:

    ```
    # esxcli network vswitch standard set -v <vswitch> -m
    <MTU_size>
    ```

    Substitute the values for <vswitch> and <MTU_size> as applicable to your infrastructure.

 MTUs for distributed switches cannot be modified from the CLI. If you need assistance with migrating VSAN networking to standard switches during outage-recovery efforts, please contact VMware Support or your third-party support provider.

 If we are using an MTU of greater than the standard 1500 bytes, upstream physical switches should be configured to handle the larger MTU. It is a valid troubleshooting step to roll back vmkernel interface MTUs to 1500 in order to determine whether it resolves the network partition. If it does, then the problem may be upstream.

12. If all vSphere-related networking settings (service tagging, MTU, VLAN, etc.) are valid and as expected, we should continue to investigate upstream. Ensure that the physical switch is configured to handle multicast IP traffic. This may require turning on IGMP snooping for the applicable VLAN, configuring IGMP queriers, or configuring other settings.

How it works...

VSAN networking needs to be consistent across all VSAN nodes to ensure proper production. For this reason, the VLAN (if any), IP subnet, and MTU must all match across hosts and MTUs must be handled properly by all vSwitches and physical Switches. To inform ESXi which interface should be used for VSAN traffic, the applicable interface must be tagged for use by Virtual SAN.

Investigating storage provider registration problems

Once you have VSAN configured and enabled, you may find that you are unable to create storage policies because VSAN storage providers are not registered. This process should happen automatically but, if the providers become unregistered, then we will need to force the system to refresh the provider registrations before VSAN policies can be created, modified, or applied.

It is likely that there is a provider registration problem if the VSAN-related policy options are not present when you go to create a storage policy or if no policy information is reported for VMs/virtual disks.

Getting ready

You should be logged into vSphere Web Client as an administrator.

How to do it...

1. To validate that the storage providers have become unregistered, in vSphere Web Client navigate to **Home | Hosts and Clusters | vCenter | Manage | Storage Providers**.

2. If there are no providers registered, ensure that TCP port 8080 is open between vCenter Server and the ESXi hosts on any physical and/or software firewalls present in the infrastructure.

3. If there are no providers registered, click the orange *refresh* icon and wait for the system to query the VSAN nodes and register the VSAN providers. The providers should repopulate:

4. You should find that one ESXi host registers as the active VSAN provider and the remaining nodes register as standby providers.

5. If the refresh operation fails or if you encounter other problems, please continue to the next recipe.

How it works...

If the storage provider becomes unregistered from the SPBM service on vCenter Server, the manually invoked refresh process instructs SPBM to query any VSAN-enabled hosts for storage-provider information. If this information is found, the providers will be re-registered.

Investigating other SPBM problems

If VSAN Storage Providers are registered and appear normal, but information about VMs is not being displayed, or if you cannot apply storage policies, there may be a problem within the SPBM service. This service typically co-resides with the vCenter services on the same physical or virtual machine.

The easiest way to reinitialize SPBM and cause data to display properly is to recycle the associated services. This service runs on either the Windows or Linux varieties of vCenter Server.

Getting ready

You should be logged into vCenter Server via RDP (Windows) or SSH (Linux) as an administrator (Windows) or root (Linux).

 If you are using vCenter Appliance 6.0, you must enable the shell with the following two commands:

```
# shell.set --enabled True
# shell
```

How to do it...

1. For Windows vCenter Server, click **Start | Run**, enter `services.msc` in the resulting dialog box, and then strike the *Enter* key:

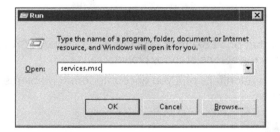

2. In the list of services, locate **VMware Profile-Driven Storage Service** and select it.

3. Click on **Restart the service** or right-click the service and select **Restart**:

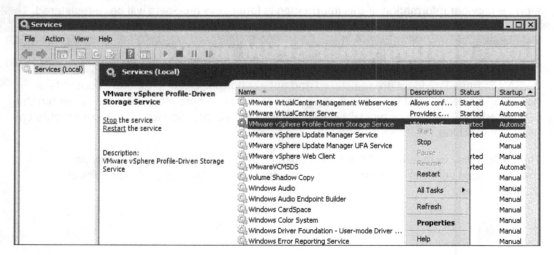

4. Log out of vSphere Web Client and log back in.

5. If you are using Linux vCenter Server Appliance, run the following command from a root shell:

```
# service vmware-sps restart
```

```
vcenter:~ # service vmware-sps restart
Stopping VMware vSphere Profile-Driven Storage Service...
Stopped VMware vSphere Profile-Driven Storage Service.
Starting VMware vSphere Profile-Driven Storage Service...Waiting for VMware vSphere Profile-Driven Storage Service........
VMware vSphere Profile-Driven Storage Service started.
```

6. Log out of vSphere Web Client and log back in.

How it works...

If SPBM is behaving unusually, forcing the service to restart will trigger a complete refresh of storage providers, applied policies, and other behaviors. Simply restarting the service to determine whether the bad behavior clears is typically fast, easy, and low-impact. Restarting Profile-Driven Storage Service will prevent the modification of the existing storage policies the application of different policies to VMs, and the creation of VM/disks with the non-default policy for the period during which the service is restarting. Once the service has restarted, all functionality will be returned. Restarting the service will have no impact on running VMs or the overall VSAN resiliency.

Investigating VM provisioning or power-on failures

If a VM fails to provision or power on, the problem is often related to degraded availability in the VSAN cluster or, more frequently, inadequate cluster storage capacity. In this recipe, we will address both of these very common provisioning/power-on failures.

Getting ready

▸ You should be logged into vSphere Web Client as an administrator
▸ You should be logged into RVC

How to do it...

Out-of-space failures

1. If the failure is capacity-related, we will see an error message in vSphere Web Client along the lines of the following:

   File [vsanDatastore] 3e192a55-c7ab-efa3-a51a-005056837d9f/linux-vm04.vmdk was not found

   The policy requires 2 replicas with 1 disks each with 42949672960 bytes free each. Only found 0 such disks.

2. In this example, we know that the policy of the affected VM involves one host failure to tolerate because the VM requires two replicas. As each replica requires only one disk, we also know that the storage policy specifies a stripe width of one stripe per mirror.

3. The VM that we are attempting to provision is 42949672960 bytes, or 40 GB, so this will be the size of each mirror.

4. VSAN was unable to locate any disk with adequate free space to provision the VM.

[This can also affect VM power-on, as VM swap objects must be provisioned at power-on.]

5. To resolve this kind of failure, we have a couple of choices. We can add physical disks, delete unused data to free up cluster capacity, or we can also make a storage-policy change to thin-provision the new VM or the other VMs already present on VSAN.

Availability-related failures

1. A VM may fail to power-on if the objects comprising it have degraded availability. This is harder to diagnose than out-of-space conditions and involves correlating more data.

2. If a VM fails to power-on because of degraded availability, you may see a message in vSphere Web Client along the lines of the following:

   A specified parameter was not correct.

   or

   "/vmfs/volumes/vsan:525e246fd7e9d76b-7c87ce4d93a74849/1cd22755-9fbe-c6a1-570e-005056831715/linux-vm03.vmdk" : failed to open (Input/output error).

3. When examining the VM's **VM Storage Policies** tab, you will find that compliance has failed and **VM Home** or **Hard disk 1** has components on more than one host in an **Absent** state:

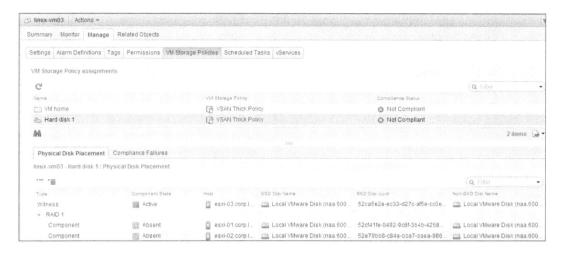

4. When running the vsan.vm_object_info command in RVC, you will find that components on more than one host are in an ABSENT state, and at least one component will report that it is STALE:

5. In this case, RVC tells us that this problem is due to a network partition. What happened in this instance is that a network partition occurred during an object rebuild, resulting in data unavailability as this became a double fault: the in-sync copy of the data became unavailable to the rest of the cluster and there was no other in-sync copy of the data available. Had the VM been affected by this problem as soon as the problem occurred, the VM would have automatically terminated to ensure data integrity.

6. To resolve this situation when there is a network partition, eliminate the network partition and a resync will begin, restoring availability. When a resync begins, it will be reflected in the **VM Storage Policies** information:

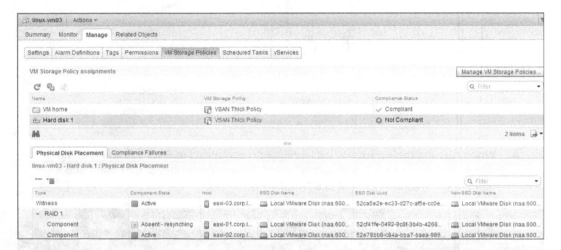

7. If the double-fault has occurred due to a physical disk failure affecting the in-sync copy of the data, contact VMware Support or your third-party support provider to discuss recovery options, if any.

How it works...

When VMs fail to power-on or provision, it is typically due to capacity or multiple faults. The messaging in either case will indicate the problem. In the case of inadequate cluster capacity, the message is very clear and describes how much space is needed to complete the operation.

In the case of degraded availability due to multiple faults, the messaging is less obvious but the tools at our disposal (such as monitoring VM Storage Policies and RVC) will help identify the source of the problem so that a solution can be determined.

There's more...

VM provisioning may fail due to capacity constraints during a clone/deploy operation. This will only happen when we are using some degree of thin-provisioning in VSAN. The reason that this can occur is that, when we clone an existing VM (or deploy a template/OVF container, and so on.) into VSAN, the objects are provisioned upfront at zero bytes. The data is then read into the object, and it grows in size as needed. If the physical disks in the VSAN cluster are fairly full and the cluster is also fairly fast, the new data can be read in faster than rebalancing operations can make space for the new size required by the object. If this occurs, then the clone operation can fail with a message about **No space left on device**.

If this occurs, then modify your storage policy to reserve the amount of space actually consumed by the source VM. For example, if the source VM is 250 GB with 150 GB used, set your **Object space reservation** policy option to reserve ~60 percent of the provisioned size and the deploy operation will succeed provided there is adequate capacity in the cluster.

Investigating disk failures

When a disk fails in VSAN, it is important to address the problem by replacing the disk. A key part of this may be determining why the failure was triggered. Determining which disks have failed is a straightforward operation in vSphere Web Client. Determining the cause of the failure will involve investigating the ESXi system logs.

Getting ready

▶ You should be logged into vSphere Web Client as an administrator

▶ You should be logged in to the affected ESXi host as the root, preferably via SSH

How to do it...

1. If you have configured VSAN alarms according to *Chapter 4, Monitoring VSAN,* when a disk fails you will be presented with an alert icon on the ESXi host and **Triggered Alarms** will reflect a disk error:

2. The failed disk will also be reflected in the **Disk Management** view:

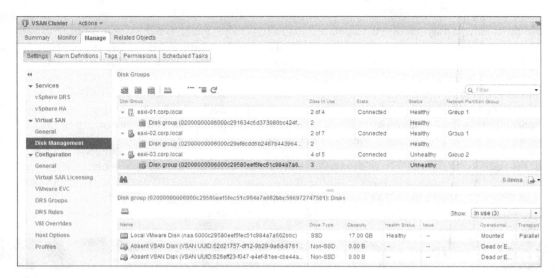

3. From here, it is fairly straightforward to remove the failed disks and replace them if desired. However, finding out why the disks have failed will require examining the applicable host's `/var/log/vmkernel.log` file to search for the cause. This requires you to log into the host via SSH or local console. SSH is recommended.

4. Once logged into the system via SSH, examine the log file by running the following command:

```
# cat /var/log/vmkernel.log |less -i
```

5. Examine the logs, specifically looking for the word *permanent*. This may be in the following form:

   WARNING: ScsiDevice: 1480: Device :<identifier> has been removed or is permanently inaccessible.

   or

   WARNING: LSOM: LSOMEventNotify:4574: VSAN device <UUID> is under permanent error

6. The preceding messages mean specific things. The first example is due to a device being removed or otherwise being disconnected from the SCSI bus. The second message will be displayed if the device is still logically or physically present, but IO processing has failed and VSAN has declared the disk as failed despite its continued presence on the SCSI bus.

7. In this example, the disks were removed and this can be seen by examining the system log:

```
2015-04-12T09:04:00.062Z cpu0:51550)WARNING: ScsiPath: 7028: Path lost for adapter vmhba0 target 2 channel 0 lun 0
2015-04-12T09:04:00.062Z cpu0:51550)WARNING: ScsiDevice: 8820: PDL set on VSAN device path "vmhba0:C0:T2:L0"
2015-04-12T09:04:00.062Z cpu0:51550)ScsiDevice: 4195: Device naa.6000c2906b54d6193f46d249b4b19284 is Out of APD; token num:2
2015-04-12T09:04:00.062Z cpu0:51550)WARNING: ScsiDevice: 1480: Device naa.6000c2906b54d6193f46d249b4b19284 has been removed or is permanently inaccessible.
2015-04-12T09:04:00.064Z cpu1:33300)WARNING: NMP: nmpDeviceAttemptFailover:566: Retry world restore device "naa.6000c2905b13e407b0c00f313a24ee43" - no more commands to retry
2015-04-12T09:04:00.064Z cpu1:33300)WARNING: NMP: nmpDeviceAttemptFailover:603: Retry world failover device "naa.6000c2906b54d6193f46d249b4b19284" - issuing command 0x412e808738c0
2015-04-12T09:04:00.064Z cpu1:33300)WARNING: NMP: nmpDeviceAttemptFailover:678: Retry world failover device "naa.6000c2906b54d6193f46d249b4b19284" - failed to issue command due to Not found (APD), try again...
2015-04-12T09:04:00.064Z cpu1:33300)WARNING: NMP: nmpDeviceAttemptFailover:728: Logical device "naa.6000c2906b54d6193f46d249b4b19284": awaiting fast path state update...
2015-04-12T09:04:00.068Z cpu1:32873)ScsiDeviceIO: 2307: Cmd(0x412e808738c0) 0x12, CmdSN 0x11b9 from world 0 to dev "naa.6000c2906b54d6193f46d249b4b19284" failed H:0x8 D:0x0 P:0x0
2015-04-12T09:04:00.068Z cpu1:32873)WARNING: NMP: nmp_DeviceStartLoop:723: NMP Device "naa.6000c2906b54d6193f46d249b4b19284" is blocked. Not starting I/O from device.
2015-04-12T09:04:00.068Z cpu1:32784)ScsiDeviceIO: 2307: Cmd(0x412e80873a06) 0x1a, CmdSN 0x11ba from world 0 to dev "naa.6000c2906b54d6193f46d249b4b19284" failed H:0x8 D:0x0 P:0x0
2015-04-12T09:04:00.068Z cpu1:32873)WARNING: PLOG: PLOG_QuiesceDevice:5203: : Got quiesce reason 1 on disk 526ef23-f047-e4ef-81ee-cbe44a127bdc
2015-04-12T09:04:00.068Z cpu1:32873)WARNING: PLOG: PLOG_QuiesceDevice:5212: Disk PDL event on device 526ef23-f047-e4ef-81ee-cbe44a127bdc when disk is already PDL
2015-04-12T09:04:00.069Z cpu1:32873)ScsiDevice: 8792: Couldn't lookup device naa.6000c2906b54d6193f46d249b4b19284
2015-04-12T09:04:00.069Z cpu1:32873)ScsiDevice: 6308: Device naa.6000c2906b54d6193f46d249b4b19284 APD Notify PERM LOSS; token num:1
2015-04-12T09:04:00.072Z cpu0:33436)PLOG: PLOGGarbageCollectDevice:920: Device naa.6000c2906b54d6193f46d249b4b19284:2 526ef23-f047-e4ef-81ee-cbe44a127bdc is prepared to delete
2015-04-12T09:04:00.072Z cpu0:33436)PLOG: PLOG_FreeDevice:230: PLOG in-mem device naa.6000c2906b54d6193f46d249b4b19284:2 526ef23-f047-e4ef-81ee-cbe44a127bdc is being freed
2015-04-12T09:04:00.072Z cpu0:33436)PLOG: PLOG_FreeDevice:313: Unregistering diskAttrHandle:0x4110c1fd5308 on disk naa.6000c2906b54d6193f46d249b4b19284
2015-04-12T09:04:00.072Z cpu1:33436)LSOMCommon: LSOM_UnregisterDiskAttrHandle:129: DiskAttsHandle:0x4110c1fd5308 is removed from moduleID 77 for disk:naa.6000c2906b54d6193f46d249b4b19284
2015-04-12T09:04:00.074Z cpu0:33436)Destroyed VSAN Slab PLOGIORetry_slab_6000000000 (maxCount=1 failCount=0)
2015-04-12T09:04:00.078Z cpu0:33436)Destroyed VSAN Slab PLOGIORetry_slab_0000000001 (maxCount=1 failCount=0)
2015-04-12T09:04:00.078Z cpu0:33436)ScsiEvents: 354: EventSubsystem: Device Events, Event Mask: 20, Parameter: 0x4110c1fd6700, UnRegistered!
2015-04-12T09:04:00.087Z cpu1:32784)ScsiDeviceIO: 2338: Cmd(0x412e80873a00) 0x1a, CmdSN 0x11bc from world 0 to dev "naa.6000c2906b54d6193f46d249b4b19284" failed H:0x1 D:0x0 P:0x0 Possible sense data: 0x0 0x0 0x0.
2015-04-12T09:04:00.34578)ScsiDevice: 1495: Permanently inaccessible device :naa.6000c2906b54d6193f46d249b4b19284 has no more open connections. It is now safe to unmount datastores (if any) and delete the device.
```

8. In the latter case, where the disk has been declared as dead because it failed to process IO, we find that there have been IO failures prior to the declaration, complete with SCSI sense data. For example:

   NMP: nmp_ThrottleLogForDevice:2322: Cmd 0x28 (0x4136c03e5e80, 0) to dev <device> on path <path> Failed: H:0x0 D:0x2 P:0x0 Valid sense data: 0x3 0x11 0x0. Act:NONE

9. This sense data can be translated to determine the reason why the IO failed (in this case, the disk returned an unrecovered read error—a physical fault).

> If the disk failure is due to an inability to handle IO rather than the device being removed from the SCSI bus, it is strongly recommended that you contact VMware Support or your third-party support provider for assistance with the analysis.

How it works...

When a disk is declared to be under permanent error by VSAN, it is always because the device has either failed completely and is no longer enumerated on the SCSI bus or because the device cannot process the IO that VSAN is demanding. Either cause has the same net effect—the disk is no longer available for use by VSAN.

If there is adequate capacity in the VSAN cluster and enough nodes, this condition will immediately trigger rebuild activity to restore the VMs to redundant protection. Replacing the failed disks then returns the cluster to its original storage capacity. If adequate capacity is not there or if there aren't enough nodes, the disks will have to be replaced or the system repaired prior to the rebuild.

See also

▶ For the disk replacement procedure, please see *Chapter 5, VSAN Maintenance Operations*

▶ For more information on interpreting SCSI sense codes, please see the VMware Knowledge Base article 289902 (http://vmw.re/1NDMPfC)

▶ For more information about what the individual SCSI sense codes mean, please see the following official T10 documentation:

❑ SCSI Status Codes: http://bit.ly/1gf037w

❑ SCSI Sense Keys: http://bit.ly/1JIbyOv

❑ SCSI ASC/ASCQ Assignments: http://bit.ly/1LMTN3P

Investigating VSAN performance with VSAN Observer

With any storage system, it is very important to be able to examine performance information and gain insight into the workload. This is particularly true for VSAN, as its distributed nature means that a VM performance problem could be due to the workload, a problematic host, a problematic disk, or other issues.

There are some options available to monitor VSAN performance in vCenter Server and VMware vRealize Operations, but VSAN also ships with a tool called VSAN Observer that can help provide information about VSAN performance. This is invoked via RVC and used via a Web browser. To use VSAN Observer in live mode (where we examine real-time data), the RVC server must have access to the Internet to assist with chart rendering.

 This recipe is not intended to be an exhaustive description of all VSAN Observer options, but it will discuss how to launch VSAN Observer and how to begin interpreting the data that it provides.

Getting ready

You should be logged into RVC as an administrator.

TCP port 8010 should be open between your workstation and vCenter Server or the machine where RVC is running.

How to do it...

1. From RVC, launch VSAN Observer for live monitoring with the command string:

    ```
    # vsan.observer --run-webserver --force
    /<vCenter>/<Datacenter>/computers/<cluster>
    ```

2. To launch VSAN Observer for live monitoring without HTTPS, use the following command:

    ```
    # vsan.observer --run-webserver --no-https --force
    /<vCenter>/<Datacenter>/computers/<cluster>
    ```

3. To launch VSAN Observer for live monitoring and record the data to a disk for later analysis, use the following command:

    ```
    # vsan.observer --run-webserver --force --generate-html-bundle
    </path/to/output/file>
    /<vCenter>/<Datacenter>/computers/<cluster>
    ```

4. For example, to launch VSAN Observer for live monitoring with no HTTPS and to save the data for later analysis:

    ```
    > vsan.observer --run-webserver --no-https --force --generate-html-bundle /root /vcenter.corp.local/Datacenter/computers/VSAN\ Cluster/
    Couldn't load gnuplot lib
    [2015-04-14 02:41:18] INFO  WEBrick 1.3.1
    [2015-04-14 02:41:18] INFO  ruby 1.9.2 (2011-07-09) [x86_64-linux]
    [2015-04-14 02:41:18] WARN  TCPServer Error: Address already in use - bind(2)
    Press <Ctrl>+<C> to stop observing at any point ...

    2015-04-14 02:41:18 +0000: Collect one inventory snapshot
    [2015-04-14 02:41:18] INFO  WEBrick::HTTPServer#start: pid=18248 port=8010
    Query VM properties: 0.07 sec
    Query Stats on esxi-01.corp.local: 1.92 sec (on ESX: 0.53, json size: 127KB)
    Query Stats on esxi-02.corp.local: 2.28 sec (on ESX: 0.74, json size: 120KB)
    Query Stats on esxi-03.corp.local: 2.50 sec (on ESX: 0.68, json size: 125KB)
    Query CMMDS from esxi-03.corp.local: 2.71 sec (json size: 53KB)
    2015-04-14 02:41:41 +0000: Live-Processing inventory snapshot
    2015-04-14 02:41:41 +0000: Collection took 22.85s, sleeping for 37.15s
    2015-04-14 02:41:41 +0000: Press <Ctrl>+<C> to stop observing
    ```

5. Once it is launched, open a Web browser and navigate to `http://<RVC server address>:8010` or `https://<RVC server address>:8010`.

> If you are using HTTPS, you will be prompted to log in. Use the credentials that you used to launch RVC.

6. Once you have navigated to the appropriate address and logged in if applicable, you will be presented with the **VSAN Client** statistics. This is the top of the VSAN IO stack on any given host and it is an "all-in" rollup of cluster performance, from the perspective of the final workload (all VMs on that host):

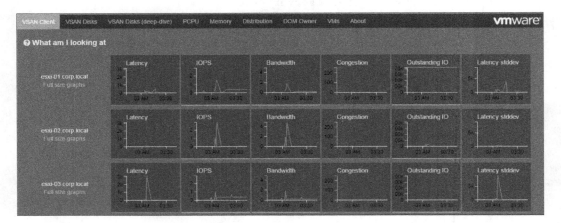

7. This will show you information about observed latency, number of **IO operations per second** (**IOPS**), how much data is being transferred, and whether VSAN is congested.

8. If the VSAN Client statistics indicate a problem such as high latency, it can be useful to click on **Full size graphs** to get a breakdown of what kind of IO is slow:

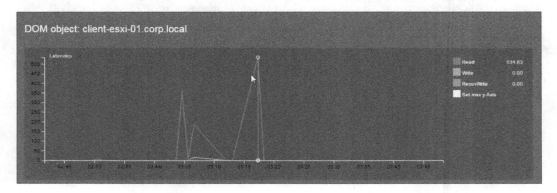

In this case, we see that the **Read** IO was slow for approximately 15 min, peaking at about **534** ms.

9. If end-user (client) latency is high, it may be useful to proceed down the VSAN IO stack and examine the VSAN disks for latency information. To do this, click on the **VSAN Disks** tab and examine the output:

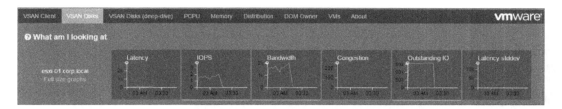

10. Here, we can see that the latency on host 01 is flagging a critical threshold because its graph is underlined in red. As before, we can get more information by drilling down into **Full size graphs**:

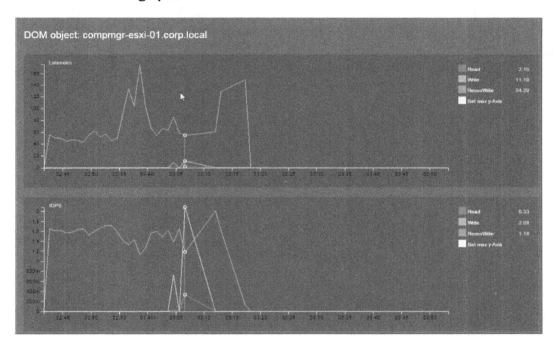

Here, we can see that most of the IOPS and latency is due to **RecovWrite**; the latency in this case is caused by object-rebuild operations, rather than normal read/write activity where latencies are still low.

11. More information about physical disk handling (such as individual device performance and cache efficiency) can be found by navigating to **VSAN Disks (deep-dive)** and selecting a host from the drop-down list:

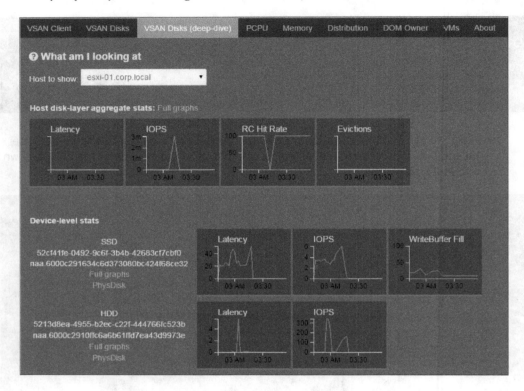

Here, we can see that the SSD latency is 20–40 ms and the read-cache hit rate is typically 100 percent, with one plunge. This indicates that the SSD is fairly slow, but the cache is generally operating efficiently.

12. To get detailed information about VM performance, navigate to the **VMs** tab and then search for or select your VM. You can drill down into individual virtual disks to see how they are performing and whether there are any obvious bottlenecks:

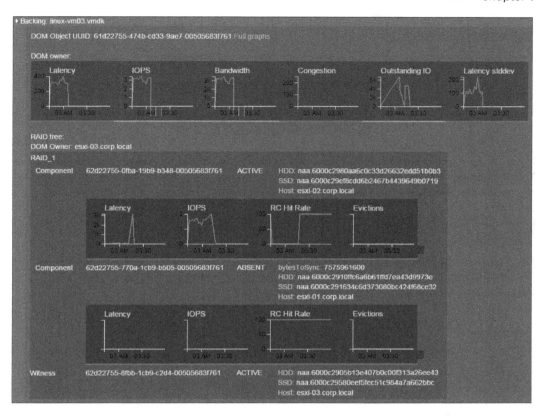

Here, we can see that latency was generally bad for some time but later improved. We can see that the component on host **esxi-02.corp.local** had a very bad read cache hit rate and very high latency. Conversely, the cache hit rate and latency were acceptable for the component on host **esxi-01.corp.local**. This implies that VM performance is affected by the poor performance on host 02.

How it works...

ESXi and VSAN continuously keep track of various pieces of performance data in nearly real time, but this data is transient. VSAN Observer methodically collects this data and renders it for analysis by using its Web-presentation engine. This information is then presented in a series of dashboards that we can navigate to gain insight into the VSAN performance at the consumer (VM), host, and disk layers of the VSAN IO stack. The data can then be compared to the manufacturer's assessment of disk performance (are the disks in production significantly slower than expected?), network speed, and so on.

There's more...

Every tab in VSAN Observer has a button called **What am I looking at**:

If you click on this button, it will toggle a description of what the metrics on that page mean. This information can be hugely useful when you first start using VSAN Observer as it helps describe what the data is and what it implies about the performance of the cluster.

See also

For a more in-depth guide to VSAN Observer, please see the VMware Technical Marketing documentation at `http://blogs.vmware.com/vsphere/files/2014/08/Monitoring-with-VSAN-Observer-v1.2.pdf`.

8
Support Success

In this chapter, we will discuss the following topics, with a recipe for each:

- ► Formulating a problem description
- ► Formulating a problem summary
- ► Collecting logging information
- ► Collecting other diagnostic information

Introduction

During the course of your VSAN deployment or during production following deployment, you may encounter a problem that requires deep, low-level troubleshooting or complex issue analysis. If this should occur, you may need to open a case with VMware Support or your third-party support provider.

As we have seen, VSAN is tightly integrated with vSphere once it is deployed, so in some ways, preparing for a support engagement with VSAN is quite similar to the regular vSphere support process. VSAN does, however, involve many elements and configuration items that are not found in non-VSAN infrastructures. To set ourselves up for success during support engagements, there are steps we can take to ensure that all the necessary data is provided up-front to avoid delays to acquire more information after the incident is raised. Properly defining the problem and providing adequate diagnostic data can help make recovering from problems and returning to production faster and easier.

Formulating a problem description

If you encounter a problem that requires you to raise a support ticket with your support provider, it is vital to clearly and concisely define what the problem is, as well as when and how you encountered it. Clarity and direction here can help prevent guesswork and provide for a speedier return to service.

 Depending on your support provider, you may not need to create both a description and a summary. If your support provider does not make use of two entries to define the incident, please proceed to the next recipe.

Getting ready

You should have some error messages available/copied, or any applicable conditions that led up to the problem in mind.

How to do it...

1. Define the problem.

   - What was going on in the infrastructure when the problem was encountered? How did you discover the problem?

   - What did the problem prevent you from achieving in your infrastructure?

2. Determine the context of the problem.

   - When you discovered the problem, was there a specific operation or any changes being made when the problem occurred?

3. Identify the scope of the problem to determine severity.

   - Are all VMs affected, just one, or a few?

   - Is the entire cluster down, or just parts of the cluster, such as during a network partition?

   - Is this affecting a production cluster? Are critical business services unavailable due to the problem?

4. Formulate the problem description.

5. When formulating the problem description, provide the necessary context without being overly vague. For example, *VSAN cluster is down* will typically be less useful than *VSAN cluster is down following site power failure*, in terms of the problem description.

How it works ...

The high-level problem description is the first thing that support personnel will see when a ticket is raised. Being clear and concise in this section and providing adequate context will help the support engineer to start determining a course of action right away, even as he or she is working through the rest of the ticket.

Formulating a problem summary

Unlike the extremely high-level problem description, the problem summary is where we should begin to address more details about the symptoms of the problem and the context surrounding when the problem began, if known.

The same rubric we used for the problem description applies here—we should be clear and concise but also build out more contexts surrounding the problem. It is in the summary that we can provide specific messaging and paint a clearer picture of the issue.

Getting ready

You should have some error messages available/copied, and any applicable conditions that led up to the problem in mind

How to do it ...

1. Determine the full context of the problem.
   - If possible, we should provide a step-by-step story of what led up to the problem.

2. Collect any error messages.
   - Exact error or notification messaging is very valuable to the troubleshooting process.

3. Examine the impact to the business.
   - What are the consequences of the problem? Is the business on the line because accounting systems are down, or are moderately-critical web services unavailable?
   - The criticality of the issue to the business is a key factor in determining resolution plans, responses, timelines, and so on.

4. Formulate the problem summary, including information about the lead-up to the problem and any messaging relevant to the issue.

5. Try not to leave out information that could be critical to routing the case to the appropriate support engineer.

    For example, a summary like this tells the story of what happened: "VSAN is offline following power failure. Production accounting systems are down."

    Despite this, we can provide greater context with a summary like: "Critical accounting systems are down following a power failure affecting the VSAN cluster. After power was restored, all VSAN nodes report that "The Virtual SAN host cannot communicate with all hosts in the VSAN-enabled cluster." Attempts to power on VMs fail due to an I/O error."

How it works...

Describing the problem including detailed messaging and impact to the business will serve two purposes. First, it will tell your support organization how critical the problem is and how quickly you need a response to restore production. Second, it will enable your support organization to properly route the ticket to the best support engineer to handle the specific problem we are facing. For example, a VSAN outage could be caused by a network problem or a storage/disk problem or a logic problem. Providing enough information to make an informed decision of how the case should be routed will help reduce the time it takes to return to service, and help prevent false starts.

Collecting logging information

System and event logs are absolutely critical to isolating the problem and determining a resolution path. Collecting this information before we file a support ticket, or very early in the process, such as while navigating the phone tree or awaiting a call-back, will help enable the support organization to work more quickly toward a resolution. Should the incident need to be escalated, or if extensive research is needed to determine the root cause, system logging data is absolutely vital.

Getting ready

▶   You should be logged in to the vSphere Web Client as an administrator

▶   If the vSphere Web Client is not available due to the outage, you should be able to log in to the ESXi hosts via the legacy vSphere Client with root credentials

▶   If neither of the vSphere Clients are available, you should be able to log in to the ESXi hosts via SSH with root credentials

How to do it...

Here, we will look at collecting logs using three different ways.

Collecting logs with the vSphere Web Client

1. In the vSphere Web Client, navigate to **Home** | **Hosts and Clusters** | **vCenter** | **Monitor** | **System Logs**.

2. Click on the **Export System Logs** button:

3. On the subsequent page, select all the hosts in the VSAN cluster and tick the box for **Include vCenter Server and vSphere Web Client logs.** Then, click on **Next**:

4. Click on the **Generate Log Bundle** button:

5. Wait for log-bundle generation to complete. Depending on the size of the vCenter Server and the inventory, this may take some time.

6. Click on the **Download Log Bundle** button. Select a location to save the information:

7. Select a location to save the system log bundles.

Collecting logs with the legacy vSphere Client

1. If vCenter is unavailable due to the issue, we may need to collect host logs via the legacy vSphere Client. Launch the legacy vSphere Client and log directly into a host, using root credentials.

2. Click on **File | Export | Export System Logs...**.

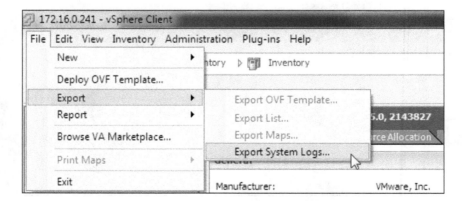

3. Leave all values at the default and click on the **Next** button.

4. Click on the **Browse ...** button and select a location to save the system log bundle and click on **Next >**.

5. Click on the **Finish** button. The logs will be generated and downloaded.

6. Repeat this process for all the hosts in the VSAN cluster.

Collecting logs via the command line with vm-support

1. If none of the graphical clients are available, we can gather system logs from the command line. Open an SSH session to the host and log in as root.

2. Enter the following command to create a log bundle and write it to /tmp:

   ```
   # vm-support -w /tmp
   ```

3. We will see the generation process as it moves through and collects system information and logging data:

```
~ # vm-support -w /tmp
06:54:51: Creating /tmp/esx-esxi-01.corp.local-2015-04-14--06.54.tgz
06:55:06: Gathering output from /sbin/vsi_traverse -s / []
```

4. When the process is completed, we are returned to a command prompt.

5. Log in to the host with an SFTP or SCP client such as FileZilla.

6. In the file-transfer utility, navigate to /tmp and download the support TGZ file.

7. Repeat this process for all the hosts in the VSAN cluster.

How it works ...

System support bundles contain more than just logging data. They also provide a snapshot of the system state, which includes statistics, configurations, hardware information and information about which VMs are registered, IP addresses, hostnames, and the ESXi-level logs for all aspects of the system. This is why obtaining this information, even if it requires the use of the legacy vSphere Client or the host CLI, is so important.

Collecting other diagnostic information

If vCenter is available, there is additional valuable VSAN information, which if collected, will help with the support process. This information can be obtained from the Ruby vSphere Console and subsequently uploaded to the support ticket.

For a refresher on how to use RVC, please see *Chapter 6, Ruby vSphere Console*.

Getting ready

You should be able to log in to RVC as a vCenter administrator.

How to do it...

Collecting VSAN support information (Linux RVC)

1. As we want to collect the support information to upload to the support organization, we will execute the RVC command as a script and redirect the output to a text file that we can subsequently upload.

2. Run the `vsan.support_information` command:

   ```
   # rvc -c "vsan.support_information /<vCenter>/<datacenter>/
   computers/<cluster>" -c "quit"
   <username>@<vCenter> |tee <filename>
   ```

3. Enter your password when prompted.

4. The output will echo to the console and be written with the filename you specified. For example:

5. This command can take several minutes to fully execute.

6. Once completed, upload the resulting file to your support organization.

Collecting VSAN support information (Windows RVC)

1. Open an administrative command prompt.

2. Navigate to the location of your RVC install.

3. Execute the following command:

   ```
   > rvc -c "vsan.support_information /<vCenter>/<datacenter>/
   computers/<cluster>" -c "quit"
   <username>@<vCenter> >> <filename>
   ```

4. Wait approximately 30-45 seconds for RVC to load in the background.

5. Enter the applicable password.

 As we are redirecting the output to a file, the **password:** prompt will not be echoed to the screen. Despite this, it will accept input and the command will run until completion.

6. This command can take several minutes to fully execute. When it is finished, you will be returned to the prompt:

```
C:\>rvc -c "vsan.support_information /172.16.0.240/Datacenter/computers/USAN\ Cluster" -c "quit" root@172.16.0.240 >> c:\vsan_support_info.txt
C:\>
```

7. Once completed, upload the resulting file to your support organization.

Collecting VSAN Observer Data

1. If we are facing a performance problem and need assistance with performance troubleshooting, VSAN Observer information can be vital to the support process.

2. To collect VSAN Observer information in a bundle that will be uploaded to the support organization, please see the *VSAN Observer* recipe in *Chapter 7, Troubleshooting VSAN*, and use the command to generate an HTML bundle.

3. Upload the resulting .tar.gz file to your support organization.

How it works...

The special RVC commands, vsan.support_information and vsan.observer, are designed to help the support organization troubleshoot a VSAN problem. These commands are analogous to a support bundle for VSAN. The vsan.support_information command will provide exhaustive details about the entire cluster, from hosts and disk information, to network configuration and object states. VSAN Observer provides crucial and detailed performance data.

9
VSAN 6.0

In this chapter, we will discuss the following topics with a recipe for each:

- ▶ Tagging disks as SSDs in vSphere 6.0
- ▶ VSAN 6.0 fault domains
- ▶ Upgrading to the VSAN 6.0 on-disk format

Introduction

The overall operational paradigm of VSAN/vSphere 6.0 is very similar to that of vSphere/VSAN 5.5. While this means that a comfortable understanding of the VSAN 5.5 release will translate directly into implementation and operations in VSAN 6.0, there are some elements specific to VSAN 6.0 that are important to understand. These include new features, such as multi-host fault domains and format upgrades, as well as improved processes related to the initial setup and configuration.

Tagging disks as SSDs in vSphere 6.0

The process of tagging SSDs via the command-line claim rule manipulation, as in *Chapter 2, Initial Configuration and Validation of Your VSAN Cluster*, was laborious. Initial Configuration has been streamlined and simplified for vSphere 6.0. This process is now possible directly from the vSphere Web Client, with no CLI interaction needed. This task is significantly faster and easier in vSphere 6.0.

Getting ready

- ▶ You should be logged in to the vSphere Web Client as an administrator
- ▶ You should know the size/capacity of your SSDs so that they can be identified

How to do it...

1. In the vSphere Web Client, navigate to **Home | Hosts and Clusters | vCenter | Datacenter | Cluster | Host | Manage | Storage | Storage Devices**.

2. Identify the SSD using its capacity or serial number and select it.

3. Click on the blue-and-white **F** icon to mark the disks as Flash. Acknowledge the subsequent dialog box:

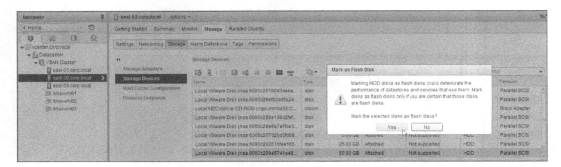

4. We will see that the **Drive Type** field changes from **HDD** to **Flash**:

How it works...

The complex process to accomplish this task in vSphere 5.5 has been automated and simplified in vSphere 6.0. When we, as administrators, are able to correctly identify which disk is the SSD in a RAID-0 configuration, tagging the disk as Flash overrides the default discovery information and allows ESXi and VSAN to use the disk as the flash device it is.

VSAN 6.0 fault domains

VSAN 6.0 introduces a feature that allows for user-configurable fault domains. As opposed to VSAN 5.5, where each host is its own fault domain, VSAN 6.0 allows hosts to be grouped together into fault domains that act as one unit for the failures-to-tolerate policy calculation.

This can be extremely useful in larger clusters or clusters that may share a common point of failure within the datacentre. For example, if we have a six-node VSAN cluster where two nodes are in each of three racks, each rack may represent a hardware failure domain because the rack may be susceptible to power-distribution failures or a top-of-rack switch failure that neighboring racks may survive. VSAN 6.0 fault domains allow us to group the hosts in such a way that we can combine hosts that are likely to fail together into a single fault domain. This can improve cluster survivability by permitting multiple node failures without affecting data availability.

As noted previously, if we opt to use user-configured fault domains, those fault domains will be used instead of hosts in the failures-to-tolerate policy calculations. As a result, if we configure fault domains, we should ensure that at least three fault domains are configured.

Like with VSAN node configurations, VSAN fault domains should be symmetrical. They should contain the same number of hosts, the same disks/disk-groups per host, the same disk capacities, and so on.

Getting ready

▸ You should be logged in to the vSphere Web Client as an administrator

▸ You should know which hosts you wish to group into distinct fault domains

How to do it...

1. In the vSphere Web Client, navigate to **Home | Hosts and Clusters | vCenter | Datacenter | Cluster | Manage | Virtual SAN | Fault Domains**.

2. Click on the green **+** button to define a new fault domain:

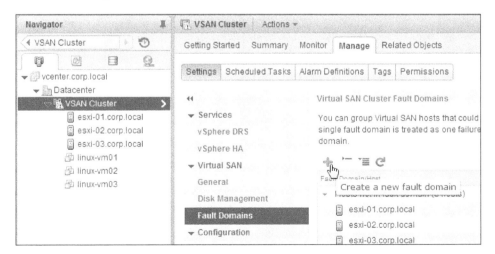

3. In the subsequent dialog box, define a name for the fault domain and select the applicable hosts. Then, click on the **OK** button:

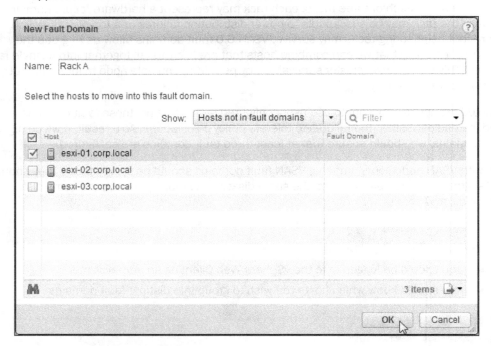

4. Repeat the preceding steps for the rest of the fault domains that need to be defined.

5. When finished, all the hosts will be associated with the applicable fault domain:

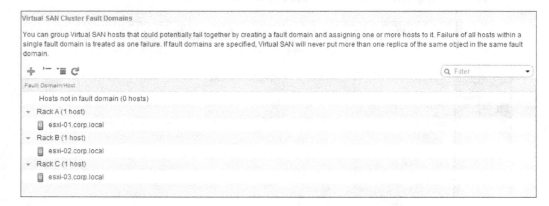

 Remember, we should define at least three fault domains.

How it works...

User-defined fault domains modify the way that VSAN determines object-placement to satisfy the *failures to tolerate* policy definition. If fault domains are not configured, VSAN will use the default behavior of treating each host as its own fault domain. When we opt to define fault domains, VSAN will distribute objects to ensure that an entire fault domain can be lost without affecting data availability. This will make VSAN more robust in infrastructures where multiple hosts may be likely to fail due to a single external event that may not affect neighboring racks or other parts of the datacenter.

Upgrading to the VSAN 6.0 on-disk format

 If VSAN was initially configured with ESXi 6.0, the on-disk format will already be current and this recipe should not be required.

In 6.0, VSAN uses a new on-disk data format. This new format is generally more efficient and handles certain VM-related activity, such as snapshots, more quickly and efficiently. The new format can also perform better on the same hardware.

For VSAN 5.5 clusters that are upgraded to VSAN 6.0, the on-disk format is not upgraded along with the ESXi version. This operation must be manually invoked after the rest of the vSphere 6.0 upgrades are complete.

This process will involve the migration of data to evacuate disk groups prior to their re-creation in the VSAN 6.0 format and/or the rebuilding of objects. As such, this operation is very I/O-intensive. It may be beneficial to schedule this operation during a period of low cluster I/O demand, such as during a weekend.

In three-node clusters that do not have two or more disk groups per host, or in clusters with little free space, the VSAN format upgrade will fail by default. During this process, VSAN attempts to proactively evacuate data to other disk groups/hosts in the cluster as this evacuation will prevent exposing any data to a potential double-fault (such as a host failure) during the upgrade process. This can be over-ridden so that the upgrade can continue, but doing so introduces a marginal risk of data loss, should there be a concurrent fault in the cluster during the on-disk format upgrade process.

Once the on-disk format operation is complete, it is permanent and cannot be rolled back. It is **strongly** recommended that production be monitored and validated on vSphere 6.0 for some time prior to making this permanent change, as this change will preclude the possibility of rolling back to ESXi 5.5.

Similarly, we should ensure that backups are present, available, and tested prior to executing this operation. The operation is safe and validates at multiple stages, but it is a significant and profound modification to the infrastructure and backups should be validated prior to execution.

Getting ready

- ▶ You should be logged in to the vSphere Web Client as an administrator
- ▶ You should be logged in to RVC as an administrator
- ▶ All VSAN hosts should be ESXi 6.0
- ▶ All critical data should be backed up

How to do it...

1. If the cluster has been upgraded to ESXi 6.0 but the VSAN on-disk format is still VSAN 5.5, an alert will be triggered in vCenter on the VSAN cluster. To identify this alert, navigate to **Home** | **Hosts and Clusters** | **vCenter** | **Datacenter** | **Cluster** | **Monitor** | **Issues** | **All Issues** in the vSphere Web Client.

2. You will find a message that indicates that one or more hosts requires a format upgrade:

3. Additionally, the VSAN Disk Management view will reveal the on-disk format version used by the various disk groups when you navigate to **Home | Hosts and Clusters | vCenter | Datacenter | Cluster | Manage | Settings | Virtual SAN | Disk Management**:

4. Once the disk version is validated as in need of an upgrade, log in to RVC as an administrator.

5. Run the following RVC command to execute the format upgrade:

```
> vsan.v2_ondisk_upgrade
/<vCenter>/<Datacenter>/computers/<Cluster>
```

6. For example:

```
> vsan.v2_ondisk_upgrade /vcenter.corp.local/Datacenter/computers/VSAN\ Cluster/
```

7. In clusters with inadequate free space or too few fault domains or disk groups, the upgrade process will fail because the existing disk group cannot be evacuated. The failure message will be **RemoveDiskMapping <host>: SystemError: A general system error occurred: Failed to evacuate data for disk uuid <identifier> with error: Out of resources to complete the operation.** To permit exposure to a double-fault during the upgrade process, please add the `--allow-reduced-redundancy` flag to the RVC upgrade command:

```
> vsan.v2_ondisk_upgrade --allow-reduced-redundancy
/<vCenter>/<Datacenter>/computers/<Cluster>
```

8. For example:

```
> vsan.v2_ondisk_upgrade --allow-reduced-redundancy /vcenter.corp.local/Datacenter/computers/VSAN\ Cluster/
```

9. As the process proceeds, progress will be echoed to the console:

```
> vsan.v2_ondisk_upgrade --allow-reduced-redundancy /vcenter.corp.local/Datacenter/computers/VSAN\ Cluster/
+-------------------+-----------+-------------+----------------+----------------+
| Host              | State     | ESX version | v1 Disk-Groups | v2 Disk-Groups |
+-------------------+-----------+-------------+----------------+----------------+
| esxi-01.corp.local | connected | 6.0.0      | 1              | 0              |
| esxi-02.corp.local | connected | 6.0.0      | 1              | 0              |
| esxi-03.corp.local | connected | 6.0.0      | 1              | 0              |
+-------------------+-----------+-------------+----------------+----------------+

2015-04-17 03:21:04 +0000: Running precondition checks ...
2015-04-17 03:21:08 +0000: Passed precondition checks
2015-04-17 03:21:08 +0000:
2015-04-17 03:21:08 +0000: Target file system version: v2
2015-04-17 03:21:08 +0000: Disk mapping decommission mode: ensureObjectAccessibility
2015-04-17 03:21:17 +0000: Cluster is still in good state, proceeding ...
2015-04-17 03:21:17 +0000: Enabled v2 filesystem as default on host esxi-01.corp.local
2015-04-17 03:21:17 +0000: Removing VSAN disk group on esxi-01.corp.local:
2015-04-17 03:21:17 +0000:     SSD: Local VMware Disk (naa.6000c291634c6d373080bc424f68ce32)
2015-04-17 03:21:17 +0000:     HDD: Local VMware Disk (naa.6000c2910ffc6a6b61ffd7ea43d9973e)
2015-04-17 03:21:17 +0000:     HDD: Local VMware Disk (naa.6000c2910ffc7f5432993487800c5911)
2015-04-17 03:21:17 +0000:     HDD: Local VMware Disk (naa.6000c29c979e0206426c5cc1267b6b86)
RemoveDiskMapping esxi-01.corp.local: success
2015-04-17 03:22:09 +0000: Re-adding disks to VSAN on esxi-01.corp.local:
2015-04-17 03:22:09 +0000:     SSD: Local VMware Disk (naa.6000c291634c6d373080bc424f68ce32)
2015-04-17 03:22:09 +0000:     HDD: Local VMware Disk (naa.6000c2910ffc6a6b61ffd7ea43d9973e)
2015-04-17 03:22:09 +0000:     HDD: Local VMware Disk (naa.6000c2910ffc7f5432993487800c5911)
2015-04-17 03:22:09 +0000:     HDD: Local VMware Disk (naa.6000c29c979e0206426c5cc1267b6b86)
AddDisks esxi-01.corp.local: success
2015-04-17 03:22:21 +0000: Done upgrade host esxi-01.corp.local
2015-04-17 03:22:24 +0000:
2015-04-17 03:22:25 +0000: Cluster is still in good state, proceeding ...
```

10. When the process completes, **Done VSAN Upgrade** will echo this to the console.

11. Once the process completes, return to the vSphere Web Client and you will find that the cluster alert has cleared and the VSAN disk groups are now reporting disk format version 2:

How it works...

Because the VSAN disk-format upgrade is a significant change to how data is handled within VSAN, the upgrade process requires a complete removal of disk groups, after which the disk groups are subsequently rebuilt. This process is orchestrated by the RVC command, including migration of data and/or object rebuild activity. The upgrade is validated and monitored as it proceeds, to ensure that no unrecoverable errors occur. If an error is encountered, the process will be rolled back to the old on-disk format. Once the process completes, however, this rollback is no longer possible. When finished, VSAN will use its new, optimized format for both disk groups and objects.

Chapter-specific Expansions

Chapter 1 – VSAN Capacity Planning

As VSAN is a policy-driven storage solution, there is no RAID configuration at the datastore level. All reliability/availability decisions, performance reservations, and so on, are made on a per-VM basis.

Because there is no datastore-level RAID decision being made, VSAN capacity and calculations are based on raw capacity. If you build a VSAN configuration of four nodes with three 2TB HDDs each, the raw capacity of the VSAN datastore will be approximately 24TB.

Capacity will be consumed according to the availability policy specified for each VM. The most typical case is a per-VM mirror. This means that, for the vast majority of all VMs running on VSAN, the datastore usage will be double that of the VM's capacity requirement.

By default, VMs on VSAN are thin-provisioned. You can choose thick-provisioning on a sliding-scale basis (from 0 percent thick to 100 percent thick), and your policy decisions here will also affect the datastore consumption.

Best-practice limits to space consumption

1. You should not plan on consuming 100 percent of the available capacity in the VSAN datastore. It is strongly recommended that you maintain 20 percent free space in the cluster. This is important as VSAN rebalancing and placement decisions need some capacity available to move objects around to optimize space distribution. To determine the ideal raw capacity, you should calculate it as <required capacity>/0.80. If your needs project that you will need 10TB of storage, consider sizing your VSAN cluster accordingly:

2. 10TB of VM usage, where VMs are protected against disk or node failure, will mean that those VMs are mirrored, so the actual raw capacity need is 20TB.

3. To comply with the 80 percent rule, take *20/0.80 = 25*.

4. You should size your VSAN to cluster to be about 25 TB.

Data working set size and capacity-tier sizing

While the arithmetic outlined in the previous section is needed to determine the raw capacity target for your VSAN cluster, the surplus capacity mandated by the 80 percent rule needn't necessarily be included in your SSD sizing decision. As the SSD is used for write buffering (and for read caching in hybrid VSAN implementations), it can be sized according to the expected size of your data set. You can calculate your SSD requirement by finding 10 percent of your expected working set as `<working set size>*0.10`.

In the context of the preceding example, the expected working set is 20TB, so the SSD sizing for the cluster is *20TB*0.10 = 2TB*.

On a gross-capacity basis, that means the SSD is only 8 percent of the raw capacity of the cluster, which is lower than the recommended 10 percent. This is okay, however, because it is 10 percent of the size of the working set.

Cluster symmetry

The previous examples are for the cluster as a whole. Cluster nodes should be symmetrical (for example, the same raw capacity for each node) and the SSD should be sized appropriately on a *per disk-group* basis.

Continuing with the example of a 20TB raw capacity need, if you were to build a four-node VSAN cluster, one possible distribution would be as follows:

▸ Four nodes with one disk group each

▸ Three 2 TB HDDs per disk group

▸ One 600 GB SSD per disk group

That leaves the cluster with 24TB raw capacity (3*2*4). In most cases (especially with some degree of thin-provisioning), this will comply with the 80 percent rule and the SSD will be 10 percent of the gross raw capacity of the cluster. This means the SSD is slightly oversized (>10 percent of the anticipated working set), but the next most common size (500GB) would be only 7.5 percent of the working set, which is too low.

In addition, such a configuration is perfectly symmetrical across nodes and this is ideal for VSAN object distribution. This configuration will also scale well, as an additional disk group could be added to each host in the future, growing capacity while maintaining symmetry, and without running out of available disk positions on most SAS controllers.

Other considerations

Most SAS controllers have eight available disk positions, discounting the use of SAS expanders. Carefully planning your disk count and capacity can make future expansion easier by enabling the simple addition of an additional, identically-scaled disk group in each host.

Chapter 2 – HA requirements for VSAN enablement

During the initial VSAN configuration, we went through the process of disabling and then re-enabling vSphere HA on the VSAN cluster. This step was necessary due to changes in how vSphere HA works in VSAN-enabled clusters.

HA behavior in non-VSAN clusters

In non-VSAN infrastructures, vSphere HA uses the host management network to determine network isolation. The hosts communicate with each other over the management network and the hosts communicate with the default gateway periodically. If this communication fails, vSphere HA determines that the ESXi host is isolated and will take corrective action.

vSphere HA datastore heart beating adds another layer of communication via the shared datastores but does not change the fundamental network-related assumptions.

HA behavior in VSAN clusters

Within a VSAN cluster, however, certain HA assumptions must change. As opposed to the typical case where host manageability is the paramount networking consideration, within VSAN the VSAN cluster communication takes precedence. For this reason, vSphere HA had to be modified to cooperate with VSAN. When VSAN is in use, vSphere HA will use the VSAN network for its host-to-host communication.

The reason for this is fairly simple. When VSAN is in use, management network availability has no bearing on whether a VM is accessible and capable of being recovered in the event of a host failure or network partition. If the management network is having problems but the VSAN network is not, it will cause needless failovers. Conversely, if the VSAN network is having a problem that results in the isolation or separate grouping of hosts, vSphere HA must be aware of those changes. If vSphere HA continues to use the management network, it could attempt to power-on VMs on hosts where a VSAN quorum cannot be established, and because of this the HA failover will be unsuccessful.

The benefits of moving HA to the VSAN network

By moving vSphere HA to the VSAN network, vSphere HA becomes VSAN-aware. If there is a network partition that results in VM object availability on one side of the VSAN partition but not the other (by definition, this will be the case—VSAN object distribution is laid out in such a way as to ensure that the same VM cannot have a quorum in multiple partitions—see *Appendix B, Additional VSAN Information*), HA will know how to bring up the VM in the applicable partition.

This is fundamental to changing how vSphere HA functions and requires a complete reconfiguration of the vSphere HA cluster and VSAN-specific modifications to vSphere HA logic. It is for this reason that VSAN cannot be enabled on a vSphere HA-enabled cluster. Once VSAN is enabled, vSphere HA can be rebuilt under its new set of operating assumptions.

Chapter 3A – VSAN-specific storage-policy options

VSAN provides multiple storage-policy options to help you define the best operating parameters for your VMs. They are described in detail here.

Number of failures to tolerate

This policy option defines how many node failures your object should survive (or how many fault domains can be lost in vSphere 6.0). Node-failure tolerance is achieved by building mirrors of your objects. Those mirrors are distributed throughout the cluster in such a way that the specified number of hosts can fail. To accomplish this, VSAN will create $n+1$ copies of the data, where n is the number of failures to tolerate.

Limitations

As quorum-based availability for an object requires that >50 percent of all data components and witnesses be available (see *Appendix B, Additional VSAN Information*), specifying more failures to tolerate requires a larger number of hosts. While VSAN will create $n+1$ copies of the data, it requires $2n+1$ nodes with storage capacity to be available to ensure that the >50 percent rule is not violated. Specifying two failures to tolerate requires $(2(2)) + 1$ nodes, or five nodes in the VSAN cluster.

Regardless of the number of hosts in the cluster, there is a failure-to-tolerate limit of three nodes.

Number of disk stripes per object

This policy option defines how many physical hard disk drives (spindles) should be used for each mirror copy of the data. This is analogous to traditional RAID-0. Striping across multiple spindles can help improve performance at the cost of additional complexity within an object.

Limitations

VSAN will limit the number of stripes we can define by policy to an absolute maximum of 12 stripes.

It is important to note, however, that the number of stripes we can define in any given infrastructure may be lower than the 12-stripe absolute maximum. As we are specifying the number of physical drives that should be consumed, we cannot specify more stripes than we have physical disks. If we have only four disks per host in the capacity tier, for example, and we want to have the fault-tolerance to survive a node failure in a three-node cluster, the maximum number of stripes we can define will be four.

Object space reservation

This policy option lets you specify whether you want the resulting VSAN object to be thin-provisioned, thick-provisioned, or somewhere in between. As opposed to "thin" or "thick" provisioning being a binary choice on traditional storage platforms, within VSAN there is a sliding scale for thick provisioning. You can specify any whole-percentage value for this policy option, between 0 percent (completely thin) and 100 percent (completely thick).

Limitations

There are no limitations to this.

Force provisioning

This policy option lets you specify whether or not VSAN is permitted to violate the specified policy in order to create the object. By default, this option is set to no for most object types. Force provisioning can be useful if, for example, you ordinarily thick-provision your VMs but you are approaching a capacity limitation in the cluster pending the installation of additional disks/disk groups or hosts.

Limitations

Technically, none. It is important to note, however, that using this policy option will permit VSAN to violate any other policy options you have specified. This option should be used sparingly and carefully.

Flash read cache reservation

This policy option lets you reserve SSD read cache for the object, as a percentage of the object's size. This can be useful for VMs or objects facing significant read performance constraints but misuse of this policy option can crowd out other IO and cause serious negative consequences in the VSAN cluster.

Limitations

The size of the SSD read cache (70 percent of the size of the SSD).

While the preceding restriction is the only technical limitation, it is important to understand how the use of this policy option can affect the VSAN cluster. As the cache reservation is a function of the object's size rather than the cache's size, it is very easy to accidentally overprovision cache reservations and starve other objects (or even the object itself, in extreme cases) of cache resources.

If you have a 100GB SSD drive, for example, 70GB of it will be used for read cache. If you specify a storage policy with a 10 percent cache reservation and apply it to two 500GB virtual disk objects, you have immediately overprovisioned your available cache on any given node and cluster performance will severely suffer.

This policy option should be used sparingly and only to address a performance problem with specific VM disks. *This policy option should not be used by default.*

Chapter 3B – VSAN Default Storage Policy

If you choose not to apply any storage policies to your VM or use a deployment mechanism that is not storage-policy-aware (such as some third-party tools or the legacy vSphere Client), those VMs will receive the VSAN default policy. The VSAN default storage policy has the following characteristics:

- ▸ 1 failure to tolerate
- ▸ 1 disk stripe per object
- ▸ 0 percent object space reservation
- ▸ 0 percent flash read cache reservation
- ▸ No force provisioning

Chapter 6 – vCenter inventory layout in RVC

The RVC directory structure will mirror the vCenter inventory tree. There are several ways to get to various points like hosts, switches and VMs. Please see the following flow charts for a breakout of the various tree structures in RVC.

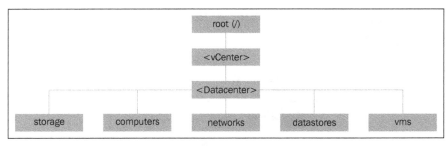

RVC root branches

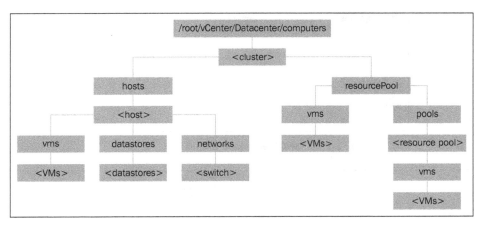

RVC "computers" branches

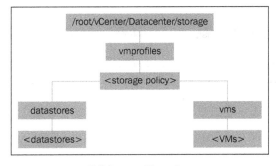

RVC "storage" branches

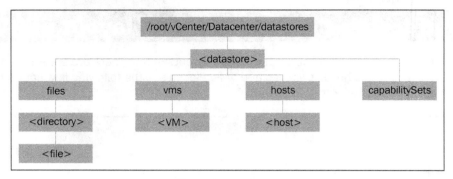

RVC "datastores" branches

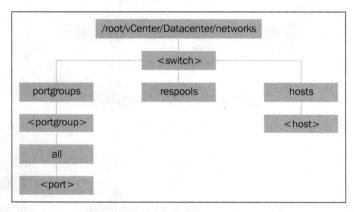

RVC "networks" branches

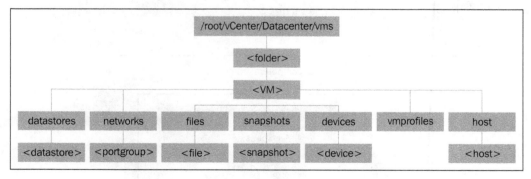

RVC "vms" branches

B

Additional VSAN Information

VSAN network considerations

As a distributed storage layer, VSAN is exceedingly dependent on robust and reliable networking. In keeping with this, VSAN requires specific networking configurations and some non-mandatory optimizations that can be put in place to improve VSAN's performance and reliability. This appendix will discuss these considerations.

Uplinks

For redundancy and reliability, the VSAN vmkernel network interface should be backed by at least two network adapters.

For host configurations with comparatively few NICs (such as hosts with the straightforward and common 2x10GbE configuration), the VSAN portgroup should be able to access both interfaces.

If bandwidth management is a consideration (for example, to balance VSAN network demands against management and VM workloads when everything shares two or more NICs), strongly consider implementing Network IO control in the vSphere Distributed Switch. Regardless of the vCenter license level, the activation of a VSAN license automatically entitles you to use the Distributed Switch for exactly this reason.

Link speed

VSAN is supported on any link speed greater than or equal to one gigabit (1GbE), although 10GbE or better is recommended.

On smaller clusters (five nodes or fewer), 1GbE networking will be adequate for production workloads. When using 1GbE networking, however, VM deployments and VSAN resync/rebuild activity will likely be network-constrained.

On larger clusters and/or extremely high-capacity clusters with significant resync-related traffic expectations during maintenance or failure, 10Gbe or better should be considered mandatory. Network traffic becomes much heavier as the number of nodes scales up, and having 10GbE becomes more important.

Link Aggregation

VSAN is fully supported in combination with link-aggregation schemes supported by vSphere ESXi. VSAN's performance can be improved, particularly on larger clusters, with the addition of link aggregation.

As data movement occurs over many unicast connections between hosts, the overall network load balances nicely as cluster utilization scales up when using link aggregation schemes, such as "Route Based on IP hash" for static port channels, or LACP when that protocol is supported by the upstream switch(es) and you are using the vSphere Distributed Switch.

The role of multicast

VSAN uses a combination of multicast and unicast traffic. Cluster-related tasks like directory services, quorum maintenance, status updates, inventory management, and so on, use multicast to minimize the amount of bandwidth consumed by these tasks. For this reason, all nodes in the VSAN cluster must be connected to a physical switch capable of processing multicast traffic. Many modern switches can automatically adjust to multicast demands and self-configure. Other switches may need to have IGMP snooping enabled. Some may need complete manual configuration of IGMP groups and queriers.

It is well worth it to take the time to properly configure and validate physical-switch multicast configuration requirements before VSAN is enabled.

The role of unicast

No VSAN production data is transmitted using multicast. When quorum is formed against an object and synchronous replication begins, the host-to-host communication for any given object, and the data movement required to service it, will occur over unicast. Many unicast connections will be made between hosts to accommodate object-level production.

Jumbo frames

Jumbo frames can provide a nominal performance boost to VSAN deployments by reducing the packet and frame overhead. It is important to note, however, that not all network interfaces and drivers support jumbo frames for multicast, even if they do for unicast traffic.

If you are planning to use jumbo frames in your VSAN infrastructure, ensure that the configuration is absolutely consistent across all nodes and physical switches. It is also strongly recommend that you perform extensive validation and testing before rolling out to production, if jumbo frames are to be used.

VSAN object distribution

VSAN objects are distributed throughout the VSAN cluster, constrained according to user-defined or default storage policies. Objects will be distributed in such a way that quorum can only be maintained on one side of a network partition, should one occur. This means that, although the VSAN cluster itself might split-brain, no VSAN object can do so, and thus data integrity is maintained across all failure scenarios. If necessary, VSAN will take an object offline (resulting in data unavailability) rather than risk a split-brain scenario that could result in corrupt or inconsistent data.

When VSAN objects are created, the various components of that object will be placed in the best possible location in accordance with policy. If multiple stripes are defined by policy, for example, they are guaranteed to be on different platters, but needn't be on the same host(s). If you have specified the fault-tolerance of a single node and two stripes, and there are greater than six nodes in the cluster, every stripe could theoretically be placed on different hosts with no impact to availability in the event of a single host failure. This allows VSAN to be extremely flexible with component placement while maintaining object availability during failure and maintenance scenarios.

vCenter object distribution view and VM snapshots

Due to interface layout constraints, only the top layer of a snapshot chain is reflected in the *Physical Disk Placement* view in the vSphere Web Client. If there is a base disk and the VM is running on a single snapshot, it is the snapshot's physical disk placement that will be reflected, not the base disk's.

Placement information for the entire active snapshot chain is available via the **Ruby vSphere Console** (**RVC**). For more information about RVC, please see *Chapter 6, Ruby vSphere Console*.

Understanding VSAN striping

While you can specify the number of stripes per object, the specification you make in that policy option is a minimum requirement. There are a number of reasons why VSAN may determine that it needs additional stripes over and above what you have specified by policy. Large objects need to be striped by virtue of the VSAN architecture. Additionally, no VSAN component can span more than one physical disk. If the overall levels of free space on any given disk are small, or if the physical disks are of a very low capacity, VSAN may need to implement additional stripes in order to build the object.

Finding that an object has more stripes in a mirror than you have specified by policy is not a cause for alarm and is completely to be expected.

The key difference between the stripes you specify by policy and the stripes implemented by VSAN for internal purposes relates to rules surrounding how those stripes can be placed. When you specify some minimum number of stripes by policy, those stripes must reside on separate physical disks. If VSAN determines that it needs more than your specified number of stripes, it can place multiple stripes on the same physical disk, as long as any failure-tolerance and explicit striping rules are not violated.

Per object quorum in VSAN

Quorum is achieved by the addition of one or more zero-length *witness* components for each object. As quorum is defined as >50 percent availability, there must be greater availability than the components strictly required to provision each mirror (for example, a simple mirror with no striping will result in two data components; as ½ is exactly 50 percent, the >50 percent quorum rule cannot be maintained with data components alone). The voting difference in a per-object quorum is made up by witness components. Witnesses are pure metadata, with no production IO being serviced. As such, they consume no space on-disk and are comparatively cheap in terms of overhead. VSAN will create as many witnesses as necessary to ensure the availability per policy in the event of a network partition or host failure affecting less than or exactly the number of nodes defined in the storage policy for the object(s).

In VSAN 6.0, witness behavior can be slightly different from the behavior in VSAN 5.5. In 6.0, each component, including witnesses, may be allocated >1 vote in the quorum. In this way, VSAN 6.0 objects may have a smaller number of witnesses than equivalent VSAN 5.5 objects. In some rare circumstances, typically associated with numerous stripes and a large number of nodes, VSAN 6.0 may not require that any witnesses be allocated.

VSAN object availability to the end consumer of storage resources (the VM) is dictated by quorum management on a per-object level. The logic is superficially simple: if >50 percent of components (data components and witnesses) and at least one complete mirror are available within the network partition, the object is available in that partition. If those constraints cannot be met, then the object will be held offline to prevent possible data corruption.

VSAN synchronous I/O flow

Assuming a healthy cluster where all members are online, all IO to an object is completely synchronous. When a `WRITE` operation is executed, the acknowledgement is not sent back to the writer until the write has been acknowledged as written into the SSD write buffer associated with the disk groups where the object's various components reside. Reads will be serviced from whichever mirror/read cache is most convenient.

In this way, data consistency is absolutely and aggressively maintained across the entire distributed object. As a result of this logic, any given mirror can fail and production will resume seamlessly with no loss of data or on-disk consistency.

VSAN object resynchronization

When a node fails and then recovers (such as in the event of a power or component failure, or if it is offline to perform system maintenance or patching), a catch-up resync operation begins to bring both mirrors into mutual consistency. It is only when this operation completes that the cluster can then fail in any direction while maintaining production.

If a node that is offline does not recover within 60 minutes, the object will be rebuilt with the available resources (assuming that those resources exist and the rebuild can satisfy policy constraints) to restore redundancy. Returning the failed node to the cluster will subsequently return space (capacity) to the VSAN cluster, but it will not immediately trigger additional resynchronization/rebuild activity.

VSAN cluster expansion

In addition to the online addition and subtraction of disks in VSAN, nodes can be added and subtracted online. If you wish to add more nodes to an existing VSAN cluster (a scale-out operation), the procedure is not profoundly different to the initial setup process. Once a node is added, the VSAN cluster has been expanded, and new provisioning can immediately make use of the new capacity. Storage capacity load-balancing will occur over time. vSphere DRS and HA can also make immediate use of the new node for resource scheduling and failure recovery.

Adding a node to the VSAN cluster

Once you have acquired the new hardware and installed ESXi, you simply to need to add the host to the vCenter datacenter. Then, create a vmkernel network interface for the new node and tag it for use by VSAN (see the *Configure VSAN Networking* recipes in *Chapter 2, Initial Configuration and Validation of Your VSAN Cluster*). If necessary, tag SSDs (see the *Tagging disks as local solid-state drives* recipes in *Chapter 2, Initial Configuration and Validation of Your VSAN Cluster* or the *Tagging disks as SSDs* recipe in *Chapter 9, VSAN 6.0*). Once this is done, drag the host into the VSAN cluster and vCenter will instruct the node to join the existing VSAN cluster.

Node addition and auto-claim

If your VSAN cluster uses auto-claim mode for disks, the disk groups will be formed automatically. If your VSAN cluster uses manual-claim mode for disks, you will need to specify which disks should be used for VSAN (see the *Manually claiming disks for use by VSAN* recipe in *Chapter 2, Initial Configuration and Validation of Your VSAN Cluster*).

Rebalancing after node addition

When new capacity and/or nodes are added to the VSAN cluster, VSAN's placement and load-balancing logic will ultimately engage in rebalancing operations and will move components throughout the cluster according to its internal logic. This is not, however, an on-demand or user-invokable process in VSAN 5.5. It will happen automatically. In VSAN 6.0, there are ways to invoke a proactive rebalance operation using the RVC command set.

VSAN rebuild logic and thresholds

VSAN object rebuilds due to a disk fault or failure

Internally, VSAN will initiate a rebuild of degraded components according to a schedule or in the event of a failure. Should a disk or disk group fail, the components on the affected disks will be immediately rebuilt if there is adequate capacity and enough nodes to comply with the policy decisions applied to the affected objects.

VSAN object rebuilds due to extended outage

In the absence of a physical fault, VSAN implements rebuild logic according to internal timers. When a node goes offline and exits the cluster, VSAN will take no action for 60 minutes. After one hour has passed, VSAN will assume that the node has exited permanently or semi-permanently and will begin to rebuild any degraded objects to restore fault-tolerance to the cluster. Re-entry of the node will not be forbidden, nor will it cause any problems.

VSAN object rebuilds during maintenance

The cluster departure timer is not disabled during maintenance operations. A powered-on/functional host in maintenance mode is in a decommission state, but it is still part of the cluster. Once the host goes down, however, the timer kicks in and the components associated with the host go into an ABSENT state. After 60 minutes elapse, even if the host was in maintenance mode, the rebuild will begin. For this reason, if the maintenance-related outage will be extended (such as during significant or lengthy hardware changes), it is recommended that all data be migrated off in advance as a part of the maintenance mode operation.

RVC scripting and redirects

As RVC provides its own shell, standard *NIX shell structures likes pipes, redirects, and loops are not available. This makes scripting RVC operations and redirecting outputs more difficult than in a standard *NIX or Windows command shell.

Due to these difficulties, it is easiest to record a session output using PuTTY or another terminal emulator if using SSH to a Linux-based RVC instance. For Windows, copying and pasting to a text file is a possibility.

Executing RVC operations as a single command

To execute RVC commands in this manner, the command syntax is as follows:

```
rvc <username>@<domain>:<password>@<vCenter_address> -c "<commands>"
```

For example, to run the vsan.disks_stats command, the command line will be the following:

```
rvc <username>@<domain>:<password>@<vCenter_address> -c
"vsan.disks_stats /<vCenter>/<datacenter>/computers/<cluster>"
```

As RVC is formally launching and logging in, it will remain logged in after the command-execution finishes. For this reason, it is recommended that you add the quit command to any command executed with the -c flag. Multiple commands can be passed to VSAN serially by the addition of more -c flags.

For example, to run the vsan.disks_stats command followed by the vsan.check_limits command and then quit, the command line will be the following:

```
rvc <username>@<domain>:<password>@<vCenter_address> -c
"vsan.disks_stats /<vCenter>/<datacenter>/computers/<cluster>" -c
"vsan.check_limits /<vCenter>/<datacenter>/computers/<cluster>" -c
"quit"
```

Redirecting RVC output to a file

To redirect the output from RVC commands, those commands must be invoked with RVC itself, and provided as a single command, as outlined previously. The output will then go to standard out and can subsequently be redirected to a file, or be piped, according to standard conventions in your shell.

Avoiding the use of plain-text passwords in the RVC command

If you do not wish to have the password revealed in plain text, it can be omitted, but this adds complication to the command. If you do not supply the password, you will still be prompted to enter it. If using a standard *NIX or Windows redirect, however, the prompt for the password will also be redirected and it will be invisible. If you choose to execute a redirect without providing a password on the command line, you can wait a few seconds and then type the password and strike *Enter*. This will be accepted by the command and it will subsequently execute.

If using a Linux version of RVC, this can be mitigated to some degree by the `tee` command, if it is available. `tee` redirects output to the file of your choice, but also echoes the same output to the console. Through the use of `tee`, you will still be able to see the prompt for the password and redirect the output. That command line would look like the following:

```
rvc <arguments> |tee /path/to/output/file
```

The `tee` command is available in the vCenter Server Appliance.

Third-party utilities

As many storage controllers are not pass-through enabled, you must create RAID-0 devices to use existing or new disks. This can be performed in the firmware/option-ROM by rebooting the host and interacting the RAID controller configuration utility via a physical or remote console.

Some RAID controller manufacturers provide tools that can be installed on an ESXi host to help interact with the RAID controller. In some cases, this can enable you to configure RAID groups from the ESXi command line, potentially avoiding the need for reboots and subsequent rebuilds for certain maintenance operations.

 Third-party utilities are neither supported nor endorsed by VMware. Documentation for third-party utilities is provided by their respective suppliers.

Utilities for HP SmartArray controllers

For HP servers using the HP SmartArray controllers, consider using the HP custom installation image for ESXi. Their custom images typically include everything from the `hpssacli` extensions to the `esxcli` command framework. This utility can be used to query the controller and perform certain operations from within ESXi.

Utilities for LSI/Avago-based controllers

For controllers based on the popular megaRAID and SAS Fusion controller chipsets from LSI/Avago, there are utilities called `megaCLI` and `storCLI`, which can be installed on ESXi servers. This standard management toolkit was ported to ESXi, and can be used to query details about the controller and RAID groups, as well as perform certain operations from within ESXi.

Index

About Packt Publishing

Packt, pronounced 'packed', published its first book, *Mastering phpMyAdmin for Effective MySQL Management*, in April 2004, and subsequently continued to specialize in publishing highly focused books on specific technologies and solutions.

Our books and publications share the experiences of your fellow IT professionals in adapting and customizing today's systems, applications, and frameworks. Our solution-based books give you the knowledge and power to customize the software and technologies you're using to get the job done. Packt books are more specific and less general than the IT books you have seen in the past. Our unique business model allows us to bring you more focused information, giving you more of what you need to know, and less of what you don't.

Packt is a modern yet unique publishing company that focuses on producing quality, cutting-edge books for communities of developers, administrators, and newbies alike. For more information, please visit our website at www.PacktPub.com.

About Packt Enterprise

In 2010, Packt launched two new brands, Packt Enterprise and Packt Open Source, in order to continue its focus on specialization. This book is part of the Packt Enterprise brand, home to books published on enterprise software – software created by major vendors, including (but not limited to) IBM, Microsoft, and Oracle, often for use in other corporations. Its titles will offer information relevant to a range of users of this software, including administrators, developers, architects, and end users.

Writing for Packt

We welcome all inquiries from people who are interested in authoring. Book proposals should be sent to author@packtpub.com. If your book idea is still at an early stage and you would like to discuss it first before writing a formal book proposal, then please contact us; one of our commissioning editors will get in touch with you.

We're not just looking for published authors; if you have strong technical skills but no writing experience, our experienced editors can help you develop a writing career, or simply get some additional reward for your expertise.

Getting Started with VMware Virtual SAN

Build optimal, high-performance, and resilient software-defined storage on VSAN for your vSphere infrastructure

Cedric Rajendran

Getting Started with VMware Virtual SAN

ISBN: 978-1-78439-925-2   Paperback: 162 pages

Build optimal, high-performance, and resilient software-defined storage on VSAN for your vSphere infrastructure

1. Effectively understand the fundamental concepts and features of Virtual SAN.

2. Implement and administer your VMware VSAN efficiently.

3. Ensure stability and data reliability and meet service-level agreements for each virtual machine and application.

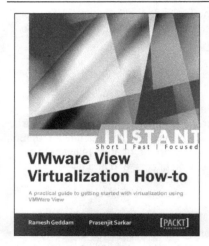

VMware View Virtualization How-to

A practical guide to getting started with virtualization using VMware View

Ramesh Geddam   Prasenjit Sarkar

Instant VMware View Virtualization How-to

ISBN: 978-1-84968-916-8   Paperback: 76 pages

A practical guide to getting started with virtualization using VMware View

1. Learn something new in an Instant! A short, fast, focused guide delivering immediate results.

2. Implement virtualization on Windows 8.

3. Learn details that are not available in the VDI documentation of VMware View.

4. Learn about the advanced features of VMWare View 5.x.

Please check **www.PacktPub.com** for information on our titles

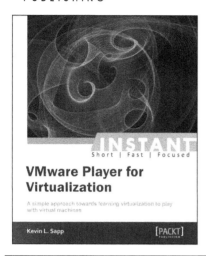

Instant VMware Player for Virtualization

ISBN: 978-1-84968-984-7   Paperback: 84 pages

A simple approach towards learning virtualization to play with virtual machines

1. Learn something new in an Instant! A short, fast, focused guide delivering immediate results.

2. Discover the latest features of VMware Player 5.0.

3. Evaluate new technology without paying for additional hardware costs.

4. Test your applications in an isolated environment.

VMware vSphere 5.1 Cookbook

ISBN: 978-1-84968-402-6   Paperback: 466 pages

Embed, display, and manage multimedia content in your Plone website

1. Install and configure vSphere 5.1 core components.

2. Learn important aspects of vSphere such as administration, security, and performance.

3. Configure vSphere Management Assistant(VMA) to run commands/scripts without the need to authenticate every attempt.

Please check **www.PacktPub.com** for information on our titles